THE MA

All about an economical and protein-packed food, including recipes for making and using tofu, soymilk, okara, go and other soybean products.

THE MAGIC OF TOFU

and Other Soybean Products

by

JANE O'BRIEN

*Illustrations by Niall Morris
and Clive Birch*

THORSONS PUBLISHERS INC.
New York

Thorsons Publishers Inc.
377 Park Avenue South
New York, New York 10016

First U.S. Edition 1983

LIBRARY OF CONGRESS CATALOGUING IN PUBLICATION DATA

O'Brien, Jane
    The magic of tofu and other soybean products.
    Bibliography: P.
    Includes index.
    1. Cookery (Bean Curd)   2. Cookery (Soybeans)   I. Title.
TX8L4.5.B4027   1983   641.6'5655   83-5083
ISBN 0-7225-0767-4

Printed in the United States of America

Thorsons Publishers Inc. are distributed to the trade by
Inner Traditions International Ltd., New York

DEDICATION

This book is dedicated to improving the quality of life for everyone.

ACKNOWLEDGEMENTS

Thank God! is the expression which really covers it all, but I would also like to thank everyone I have ever met and those people who deserve special mention as follows: my patient, understanding husband; my children, Quinn, Brett and Shane; my friends Carl Berkeley and Muriel Powell; Ken Kinsella; Thorsons Publishers; Michael Murphy; Thelma Dalman; Richard Leviton; Darrilyn Jackson; Bill Shurtleff and Akiko Aoyagi; Roisin and Sarah Curran, Diarmuid Kennedy, Paul Gannon, Des Kerrigan, Norma Redmond, Sharon Twomey and Niall Morris; Pam Tyler; David Fairweather; Philip Guiney; Stan O'Connor; Joe and Pauline Fitzmaurice and Tony and Marie Walshe; Robert Chambers and his wife Lillian; Jack and Diane Swaysland; Frank Kennedy; Patrick Mason and Stuart McDonald; O. Z. Whitehead; May Vine; Val and Tony McGinley; the Honourable Dominick Browne; Ann King-Hall; Tony and Marie Webster; Maurice Pickett; Eleanor O'Callaghan; my father, Tom Moore; my sisters, Susie and Marianne and my close and loving friends and relatives from my home town of St Louis, Missouri; Kay Boylan and May Casey; to the many people who replied to my requests for information unhesitatingly, especially Joe Rackis.

There are many other people whom I haven't mentioned and to whom I'm grateful, but this could go on forever and it is a pretty small book! I give thanks and send best wishes to you all.

CONTENTS

FOREWORD

The need for protein in human nutrition has long been recognized, and different cultures around the world have interpreted that need differently. Whether a people's diet consists mainly of animal or vegetable proteins is traditionally dependent upon that people's economic status or religious beliefs.

Recently, however, more of us are looking toward the use of vegetable proteins in our diets because there is more and more evidence that animal protein adds to or creates health problems. Vegetable protein is found abundantly in grains of all kinds, in legumes, seeds, and nuts, and by combining several of these foods in a meal one can be assured of a complete protein source which will generally contain fewer calories, less salt and less fat, and is available at a lower cost.

One of the most interesting and versatile sources of protein is the soybean. Processed into tofu and tempeh it is marvellously tasty and one has but to learn how to use it and he will become an advocate for life!

Recently a lady called at my office and asked if I would come to speak to a group of clubwomen who had read about tofu and knew it was good for them, but were 'frightened to death of it!' For those of you who might be just curious, and for those of you who are 'frightened to death', Jane O'Brien has prepared this book. Jane is known internationally for her interest in nutrition and vegetarianism and has become a respected authority on cooking with vegetable proteins. She has lectured widely and conducted cooking classes from which her recipes were developed.

Use this book with the great joy of discovery and the confidence that you will experience improved health and greater energy.

Enjoy soy!

THELMA DALMAN
Director of Food Services
Santa Cruz City Schools
Santa Cruz, California

INTRODUCTION

Tofu is curdled soybean milk, or soy curd. It is a wonderfully versatile food which has been one of the staples of the Oriental diet for centuries, and is now becoming increasingly popular in the West. Westerners are using this 'superfood' in the traditional Eastern way, but they have taken it a step further and have now developed simple recipes for many popular Western dishes which could previously be made only with animal products such as meat or dairy foods.

Tofu can be made into positively delicious 'cheesecakes' without the use of cheese or eggs; it can be fried in oil and sprinkled with natural soy sauce (as is found in natural food stores or in the natural food sections of supermarkets), and it can then be used as one would use meat. It can be made into delicious creamy sauces, dressings, mayonnaise-like products, and whipped cream substitutes; it can be added to soups, salads, scrambled eggs, waffles, pancakes and French toast, and in all of these the use of real eggs is entirely optional.

The list is endless, and each dish is more tasty than the last. With such a wide range of possible uses for tofu, it would be difficult not to find something to please everyone. I have mentioned some dishes that can be made without the use of animal products because I find it so exciting to think that a beautiful 'cheesecake', for instance, can be made without the need for cheese and eggs, since I had been led to believe that there was no alternative. Having said this, I must now mention that not only can tofu stand perfectly well on its own, but it combines beautifully with other foods such as cheese, eggs and milk, so that it is entirely up to you which way you choose to use it.

Not only is tofu fun, exciting, tasty and delicious to use in all its myriad wonderful forms, but it has many distinct nutritional advantages; it is a high-protein, low-fat, low-calorie food which is easily digestible and very inexpensive compared to other high-protein foods available today. I will go into greater detail about this subject in the chapter on food values.

Learning about tofu, and indeed about soyfoods in general, is a bit like learning a foreign language with a few new terms which soon become part of one's vocabulary. Tofu is made from thin soymilk and the process for making it commercially is really just an advanced, more mechanized version of the process for making it at home. To make soymilk, you simply grind the beans (which have been pre-soaked) into a pulp with water in a blender, then you add this slurry which is called 'go' to a large quantity of boiling water. You then pour this mixture through a cloth bag and press or squeeze the bag to extract the soymilk from the bean pulp or 'okara'. The milk is ready for use after it has been simmered for seven minutes. If you have made thin soymilk which you are going to make into tofu, the next step is the addition of a curdling agent which causes the milk to separate into curds and whey. You then pour the curds into muslin-lined settling boxes, press them for about 15-20 minutes, and you have a solid block of tofu which you may use immediately, if you wish, or store covered in water in a plastic, stainless steel or glass container in the refrigerator for future use. Tofu stays fresh for about a week if you change the water daily.

One of the real advantages of making tofu at home is that you have not only tofu, but okara and whey as well, and these are both useful products. There is nothing quite so nice as freshly made tofu which is still rather soft, warm and delicate. It is really delicious when it is simply cut into cubes and put into a salad. One of the nicest parts of making soymilk at home for use as a substitute for dairy milk is that you make both fresh soymilk and fresh okara in the process, and after simmering the milk, as it cools, you find that it develops a skin on the top, like dairy milk does, and this skin is called yuba. Yuba is considered quite a delicacy in the Far East where there are whole shops and factories devoted to making and selling it. It is very delicious when eaten from the freshly made soymilk with a few grains of salt and perhaps some raisins or honey.

Don't Be Discouraged

Don't let the recipe for making tofu discourage you, because it is really quite a simple mechanical process; housewives have been doing it for centuries, and so have 'househusbands'! You might first try making soymilk and then go on to making tofu because there are fewer steps in the soymilk making process. I started with tofu, following the directions step by step. When I became familiar with the process, after having made it once, I then made a double recipe, and when I knew how to do that, I worked out how to make six times the recipe in one session which yielded 10-12 lb (5-6 kilos) of tofu.

If you have soaked soybeans and circumstances arise which prevent you from making them into soymilk or tofu, it is quick and easy to make them into soynuts or cooked soybeans, and I give instructions on making them in this book. It simply means that you never need waste soaked soybeans.

I feel that I would be doing the soybean a severe injustice if I didn't mention some of the other foods which are being made from it. I find it rather amazing that such a bean can be made into so many wonderful foods, to say nothing of its contribution to such things as paint, printing inks, papers, glues, soaps, cosmetics and beauty aids. But here we will concentrate on foods. There is soybean oil which is used as a vegetable cooking oil and which is included in salad dressings and vegetable margarines. Tempeh is a fermented soybean food which looks like a cake of soybeans all held together by a delicate white mould — something like a cheese. It is as delicious when deep-fried, and can be cooked in many different ways; it has a flavour similar to that of chicken, and it is one of the few vegetable sources of vitamin B12.

There is soy flour which makes bread and pastries a little more moist and gives a better keeping quality. There is defatted soy flour, soy grits, soy concentrates and isolates, and spun protein fibres which come from the left-overs of the oil extraction process. The flour, grits and concentrates are used in the baking industry, in processed meats, cereals, infant foods and sweets. The isolates are used in substitutes for dairy products like powdered milk substitutes for teas and coffees, whipped cream substitutes and some forms of whipped ice-cream-style desserts. The spun protein fibres are made into meat substitutes such as textured vegetable protein. There is natto, another fermented soybean food which is easy to digest and is also another vegetarian source of vitamin B12.

In addition to all these, there is miso which is a fermented soybean food which comes in paste form and which is also a staple food in the East. It has many uses, makes delicious soups, salad dressings, and seasons all kinds of dishes and it is a valuable health-giving food which is very kind to the digestive system. There are many different varieties of miso which give subtly different flavours to food. Miso is becoming more and more popular in the West, so much so that it is now being made in America and not just imported. Once you start using it, you wonder how you did without it.

Natural soy sauce, like miso, comes in several varieties, each of which has a distinctly different flavour, and each of which makes a delicious addition to many foods. I make a wonderful French onion soup with Lima tamari simply by *sautéeing* onions in oil, adding water to more than cover the onions and adding tamari to taste. It is simple and very popular. There has been some confusion over the names applied to natural soy sauce. Apparently, in the early days when soy sauce was just being introduced in the West, the name tamari was applied to a soy sauce that is strictly speaking 'shoyu'. Now that more varieties are becoming known and available here, it is difficult to correct the original error. Original tamari was the liquid which accumulated in the miso keg during the process of fermenting miso. Tamari contains little or no wheat, whereas shoyu is made from equal parts of soybeans and wheat. In shopping for natural soy sauce, you will find some brands called tamari and some called shoyu, and it is simply a case of trying different brands to see which you prefer, and indeed of finding interesting and different uses for them all. The main point about natural soy sauces is that they are made in the traditional manner, aged for a year to a year and a half, and their flavour is superb.

I could go on and on, but this book is meant to be a simple introduction to the use of tofu, short and to the point, with an assortment of recipes, so that people who have never heard of tofu nor had any experience with it can learn not only how to use it if they are able to buy it commercially made, but also how to make it at home, if they are not. I include a selection of relatively simple recipes, and show that tofu can be easily adapted to a wide variety of dishes which will appeal to the most western of Western tastes. The recipes are meant to be guides rather than exact definitive boundaries, and you will soon learn to experiment and come up with many original and delicious recipes yourself.

My Story

Before I go on to the other sections of the book, I did want to tell you something about me, so that you may have some idea of my interest in this subject. First of all, I have always loved cooking, mainly because I have always loved eating. I remember experimenting with recipes from about the age of seven. Nobody would have called them very successful, but I did make up my own recipes for 'cookies' that ended up something like cinnamon rocks, but it was a beginning. I am quite sure that my interest was encouraged by my father who was and is a wonderful cook, and while he generally eats more simply now than he once did, he made delicious gourmet concoctions that would have tempted any palate, so I guess it could be said that he set the pattern for me in that way. Also I found that if I wanted to have the kind and quality of food that I enjoyed, I had to make it myself because others had neither the interest nor the desire.

If all had been well with me, I would have continued in the way of gourmet cooking, and I might have been writing a book on that subject now, but I was a child in America in the forties and fifties when processed foods were becoming more and more popular; at that time most people were unaware of the dangers of diets which were full of meat, sugar, refined flour products, carbonated beverages, and all the things which people who are involved with natural foods would call 'junk foods'. With all that, I was frequently ill as a child, and on several occasions I was very near to death's door. As a young adult, and even after marrying and having children, I frequently suffered from less than radiant health. It was my husband who, before he became my husband, gave me the first book on natural foods, but he had no idea how far I would take it.

As soon as I became aware that food contributed to the maintenance or destruction of health, I began a lifetime of experimentation. I changed from refined foods to whole foods, gave up eating red meat, studied macrobiotics, so much so that over ten years ago I went to Boston with two children under the age of four, and pregnant with a third, to study the subject, and I continued from there to develop my own system. I held on to the things that worked and kept working on the things that didn't, which is what I still do today. My husband is quite happy with my cooking now because over the years, it has become quite acceptable again, but you can imagine the years of transition when I changed from something of a gourmet cook, creating lovely meals according to the French, Chinese, American tradition, to what may have seemed something like a 'has-been gourmet' on an austerity programme involving giving up meat, cutting down on and nearly eliminating dairy food, getting rid of sugar and using only dried fruit for sweetening with a rare dip into the honey jar. My husband was, gratefully, long-suffering, and we got through it, but there were some pretty grim meals as I was learning.

Fortunately for them, my children were young enough with simple enough tastes to be quite satisfied and, besides they knew nothing else. Their health was good, and my health was continually improving, so I knew that I was on the right track. I have been working on creating meals that are increasingly more healthful for over seventeen years now, and I find it a fascinating study. It is so wonderful to witness the vast improvement in my own health, as well as in that of other people who make changes in their way of eating. My cooking has become so good now that I can even put together a meal which people who are not used to natural foods enjoy very much.

My children are far healthier than myself when I was growing up, and while they are now free to eat as they wish when they are out, and to have certain freedoms at home as well, I still keep my usual standard of good quality natural foods in the meals which I make at home. I know that if I made a fuss and prevented them from eating things which I consider to be 'anti-nutritional', it would make them even more inclined to eat those things, so I say nothing most of the time. I have relaxed more or less into the position of a mother of teenagers, realizing that I must relinquish my authority over them in increasingly more areas. My son, Quinn, is fifteen years old, and he enjoys meat which he has when he is out if he wishes because I don't serve it at home; he also drinks coffee with sugar, whereas I would prefer that he didn't. My daughter, Brett, is fourteen, and she won't eat meat, but she enjoys chocolate and sweets. My son, Shane, is nine, and he won't eat meat, but he also likes chocolate and sweets. Fortunately now, there are carob bars available, and that helps. My children are all really aware of the effects of 'junk foods' on them, but sometimes they prefer to ignore their awareness; it is all right as long as they feel well, but as soon as they start to feel bad in some way, they begin to eliminate or cut down on the offending foods, and doing so usually brings about a rather quick recovery.

Having said what I have about food and my interest in it and the improvement that I have made in my own health as a result of a change in diet, I must also add that I don't believe that food is the only and ultimate answer to health, but that it is one of several factors which must all be brought to the highest possible level for any individual to enjoy an exceptional quality of life. One must balance one's spiritual nature, one's mental attitude, food, exercise, career, social and family life. In the order of importance for living life to its fullest, I would say that first and foremost is the expression of our spirituality and the acknowledgement of one's dependence on that higher force which has created us. I express that aspect of my life by being a Bahá'í, and that is truly the most important element in my life. Secondly, I think that it is vital to have a positive attitude, and then I think that food is essential to earning and maintaining health.

Exercise is another important element which is too frequently ignored by people. I find that the most practical form of exercise is 'rebounding' on a small unit which is easily stored at home — it is much like a small trampoline, and it is one of the most efficient means of exercise yet developed. I put on some music and bounce, jump, jog, dance on my rebounder for about half an hour every day; it is wonderful exercise for the whole body, and I don't even have to leave my home, change my clothes or worry about the weather. There is only one cash outlay involved — the cost of the rebounder — there is no yearly subscription to a health club or sports club. I thoroughly enjoy it.

If one can come to terms with all those things while pursuing a productive career in service to mankind and carrying on a happy family and social life, what else is there? One couldn't be bored with all those interesting areas to develop.

In furthering my interest in natural foods, I have given cooking classes in Dublin for over ten years now, not steadily, but from time to time when there were people interested. In the early days of my cooking classes, I also imported the necessary foods: whole grains, beans, miso and natural soy sauce from suppliers in England as they were not available in shops here in Dublin. There was no other way of getting those foods for my family. During the cooking classes I sold much of the stock, so that friends would have access to these foods that I was using and finding so helpful and healthful. That led to the beginning of Ireland's first natural food store which I started with my husband's patient assistance, but which we left to someone else for many reasons, not the least of which was the fact that I was pregnant with another child, and I didn't fancy running a natural food store at the expense of mothering my older children and a baby. Because my husband is an actor, whose work frequently takes him away, he was not really in a position to carry on running the store and leave me to my mothering.

A few years ago, I did several series of cooking classes with a friend, and one series was held in the evening adult education programme of a local school; we even took the classes all the way across Ireland to the town of Tralee where we received a very positive response. Several years ago, I began to use tofu and soyfoods and to include them in the cooking classes. Because I was so interested in learning more about them, I attended the soyfoods conference held in Illinois in 1980 and the one in Colorado in 1981. I was also fortunate enough to visit the New England Soy Dairy in Greenfield, Massachusetts in 1980; and, during the soyfoods conference in 1981, I visited the White Wave Tofu Plant in Boulder, Colorado.

I think that I became so excited about tofu, soymilk and soyfoods really because I had long been a lover of puddings, custard and creamy topings, often made with dairy foods. However, because I needed to cut down on my use of dairy foods, I had nearly eliminated all those things from my diet. When I discovered that it was possible, not only to make tofu and soymilk successfully in my own kitchen, but to use it for very accurate substitutions of my childhood favourites which were far more healthful than the things I had eaten as a child, I was thrilled. All of a sudden, I could make puddings, custards, ice-creams, creamy dressings, mayonnaise substitutes, milk shakes, all of which turned out to be even better than the ones I had loved. Now I have settled down a bit and don't feel the need to make those things as much any more, but at least I know that I can make them if and when I want to. I have some recipes that are particular favourites which I use regularly, and my experimenting with new ways of using tofu and soymilk has added a whole new dimension to my natural food cooking which has been wonderful. It has all been quite an adventure — this quest for knowledge of how to improve the quality of life — and it continues because it has taught us so many helpful things. Our way of life may be rather unusual to many people, but one thing is for certain: it is rarely dull!

Now, enough is enough, and it is time to go onto the next phase. I wish you the best of luck, and most of all, please enjoy, enjoy, enjoy — remember that I am encouraging everyone to try to get to know tofu most of all because it is a wonderful food of which we in the West have been too long deprived, and I think that it is about time that we caught on and caught up, and in so doing we can share what the Easteners have known and enjoyed for so long; but not only that, we can show them many new and innovative ways of using their

staple food. I am sure that they wouldn't recognize tofu as tofu in
many of the dishes that we have created.

1.

MAKING YOUR OWN TOFU

Now to get down to basics. This chapter is the core of the book. I will give you instructions for making tofu for those of you who are interested because the process can give a great deal of satisfaction. It is really a simple procedure once you get used to it and understand it. By making tofu at home, you have the advantage of tasting really fresh tofu and of using the by-products of the process such as okara and whey which you don't get when you buy tofu.

The first time that I made tofu, I made sure that I had a friend with me. I asked my friend, Carl Berkeley, who has been my partner in giving natural food cooking classes, to come over so that we could make tofu together, and that gave me the moral support that I needed to get on with the job. If you are the kind of person who could benefit from such an arrangement, I heartily recommend inviting a friend over because it makes the time spent learning to make tofu more fun and takes the pressure off you to solve every question or problem on your own. It is really the timing of the matter which must be worked out, and it is easier to do this if there are two of you, at least the first time.

Equipment

Strong electric blender which can be run steadily for 1½-2 minutes without stopping (some have to be stopped periodically).

Cooking pot (5-6 quarts) with lid.

'Pressing pot' or large bowl or basin and a large, round-bottomed colander which fits into it.

Source of boiling water (saucepan or electric kettle).

'Settling box' for the finished tofu (a colander will do or a plastic container into which you have made holes for draining the whey from the curds, and a lid or a plate which fits into it for pressing the tofu. I normally put a jar of nuts or raisins on top of the plate to press the tofu). It is possible, in some places, to buy ready-made settling boxes for tofu making.

A calico bag which will serve to collect the okara and let the soymilk through. I made mine about 23 inches (58cm) wide by about 18 inches (46cm) long. I made them with French seams which I zigzagged for extra strength because they must withstand a fair bit of pressure when you press the hot soymilk through them. To make French seams, you simply put the wrong sides of the material

The two main items of equipment. On the left a colander lined with muslin into which the final curds and whey are poured, and on which a weighted plate is placed to press the tofu curds into one block of tofu. (This might as easily be a rectangular shape.) On the right is the colander lined with a calico bag into which the ground soybeans are poured from the pot for the purpose of separating the milk from the soy pulp (okara). One can make a settling box according to the final shape wanted for the finished product.

together first and sew the seams, then you turn the bag inside out and sew another seam which then encloses the raw edges of the first seam. It is the kind of seam that is often used on fine fabrics, mainly in underwear, blouses or evening wear, but it is very suitable for this purpose. Also, by enclosing the raw edges of the material, you make sure that you get no loose threads in the soymilk or the okara in the pressing process.

A piece of finely woven muslin for lining the settling box. (This should be big enough to wrap all around the tofu in the box.)

Long-handled spoon for stirring the soymilk while it is cooking.

Measuring cup.

Measuring spoon.

Ladle (or you may use your measuring cup instead).

Rubber gloves.

Ingredients

Soybeans — ¾ lb (350g or 2 cupsful), soaked for about 10 hours. (If you can get the larger soybeans, you will get a better yield of tofu.)

Nigari — 2 teaspoonsful. (This is a seawater extract used as a curdling agent which makes a fine, subtly sweet tofu. It is usually available in natural food stores and can be ordered if it is not kept in stock.) Other choices of curdling agents that may be used *instead of nigari:*

Epsom Salts (Magnesium Sulphate) — 3 teaspoonsful to 1 cupful of water yields a soft mild tofu.

Lemon Juice — 6 tablespoonsful (freshly squeezed) to 1 cupful of water yields a tangy, coarser tofu which is very tasty.

Cider Vinegar — 5 tablespoonsful to 1 cupful of water results in a slightly tart tofu which is also nicely flavoured.

Calcium Sulphate — 1 tablespoonful gives a softer, fine tofu with a higher yield. (If using calcium sulphate, you must let the soymilk cool to 160-170°F/71-76.5°C before adding the calcium sulphate all at once. You will need a cooking thermometer for this.

Soaking the Beans

Put the beans into a bowl and run cool water over them to fill up the bowl, pour the water off and refill the bowl while stirring the beans around to release the dirt. Repeat the process until you are sure that the water is clear and the beans are clean — it doesn't usually take long. Cover the beans with water in the bowl, making sure that the water is at least two inches above the beans because they absorb water and expand during soaking, and they should still be covered with water in the morning.

A word about the water temperature: If the weather is cold, soak the beans in warm water; if you have only 8 hours to soak them, then put them into hot water; and if you have only 4 hours to soak them, put them into boiling water, and after a couple of hours, pour off the water and refill the bowl with boiling water. You will have to work out the timing according to the temperature of your kitchen, and it will change as the weather changes, but soon you will understand how it works.

Note: The beans must be tested before grinding to see if they are ready, and this is done by splitting them open. If they are flat and of uniform colour in the centre, they are ready. If they are concave and darker yellow in the centre, they must be soaked for longer. As mentioned above, soaking time may be shortened by using warm, hot, or boiling water. Let me also mention that beans may be over-soaked, so *use them when they are ready.* The first sign of oversoaking is the bubbles that appear on the soaking water. I have used the beans which have had bubbles on the soaking water with no ill effect, but if I had allowed the process to continue and the soaking to go on, they would have become sour, and I am sure that the resulting tofu would have had an unpleasant taste.

When the beans are ready, and you have your equipment all laid out conveniently in the kitchen, it is time to begin:

1. Moisten the pressing sack and line the colander with it. Set the lined colander into the pressing pot.

2. Pour 3 pints (1½ litres or 7½ cupsful) water in the cooking pot and place it, uncovered, over a high heat to bring it to the boil.

3. While the water is boiling, divide the drained beans into two equal portions. Combine one portion in a blender/liquidizer with 1 pint (½ litre or 2½ cupsful) of boiling water and blend them at high speed for 2 minutes or until they are a very smooth consistency. Don't hesitate to add more boiling water to the liquidizer/blender if the machine is groaning a bit under the strain of too many soybeans. (You may have been a little generous in your measurements.) Empty the mixture into the boiling water in the cooking pot, remove the pot from the heat and cover it. Repeat the procedure with the remaining beans.

If you have no blender, you can use a hand grain mill or food mill or even a meat grinder if it will grind finely enough. Be sure, if using a hand grain mill, that it won't be ruined by grinding the moist beans. In this case, you should grind the beans as finely as possible in the mill — and it may be necessary to grind them twice, that is put the ground beans through the

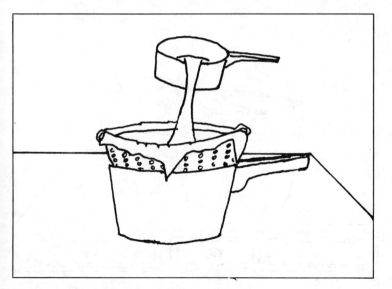

Pouring the ground soybeans mixed with boiling water into the calico bag lined colander in order to separate the milk from the okara.

mill a second time to make the grinding come out finer still —
and add the ground beans plus an extra 2 pints (1 litre or 5
cupsful) of boiling water to the cooking pot.

4. Stir the ground beans in the cooking pot, then pour the contents
   into the pressing sack or bag, allowing the milk to go through
   the colander into the pressing pot. Quickly scrub out the
   cooking pot with cold water and return it to the cooker stove.
   You might also wash out the liquidizer/blender at this point.

5. Wearing the rubber gloves, with one hand twist the mouth of
   the pressing sack closed and with the other hand, press the sack
   against the colander with a sturdy jar or potato masher or large
   spoon to extract as much soymilk as possible. I usually don't use
   anything except my hands now to squeeze out the milk, but be
   careful not to burn yourself with the hot soymilk. Shake the
   solids in the pressing sack to the bottom and press them again.

Pressing the closed calico bag of okara with a potato masher to squeeze out the last
drops of milk.

6. Open the mouth of the sack wide in the colander, stir the solids with a spoon, then add 1¼ pints (¾ litre or 3 cupsful) of boiling water and stir well. Twist the sack closed and again press as much soymilk as possible out of the pressing sack, using whatever method suits you best, again taking care not to burn yourself.

7. Remove the pressing sack and colander, then pour the liquid in the pressing pot back into the clean empty cooking pot on the cooker stove. This liquid is the soymilk. Heat it over a medium heat if stirring frequently or over a high heat if you can stir it constantly, until the liquid begins to boil. (Watch it carefully as it boils over very quickly.) Also, after it has come to the boil, it can go off simmering very easily if you are not watching it, and you must make sure that it continues to simmer for 7 minutes. If you are sure that the milk is simmering nicely and will neither boil over or stop simmering, this is a good time to clean up the colander and pressing pot with cold water and a scratchy pad. Empty the solids (okara) from the pressing sack into a plastic bag or a bowl and refrigerate them for future use in granola, baking, croquettes, soups or as animal fodder. Put the pressing bag to soak in cold water after rinsing it thoroughly. (Later, wash the bag out well in a washing machine or by hand after it has soaked in cold water for a few hours.)

8. Place the nigari or other curdling agent into the measuring cup and dissolve it completely with 8 fl oz (200ml or 1 cupful) of cold water.

9. Remove the soymilk from the heat after it has simmered for 7 minutes. With a long-handled spoon, immediately stir the soymilk vigorously a few times, and while stirring, pour in ⅓ cupful of solidifier solution (nigari, Epsom salts, lemon juice or cider vinegar dissolved in water). Continue stirring for about half a minute, being careful to reach the bottom and sides of the pot (tofu curdles from the bottom up). Now stop stirring and wait until the liquid movement ceases. Remove the spoon and pour another ⅓ cupful of the solution onto the back of the spoon, using it to disperse the solution so that it falls like rain over the surface of the milk. Cover the pot and wait for 3 minutes.

For calcium sulphate — Make sure that it is well dissolved in the water, or the tofu will taste chalky, and wait until the soymilk cools to 160-170°F/71-76.5°C before adding it. (You will need a cooking thermometer for this.) The calcium sulphate must be added all at once and then stirred in well. Cover the pot and let it stand for about 6 minutes, then proceed to step 11. If you have been using calcium sulphate and find that your tofu is too soft, use more calcium sulphate and stir it thoroughly.

10. *This is the next step if you are using nigari, Epsom salts, lemon juice or cider vinegar:* Stir the remaining solidifier solution, remove the pot lid and, using the back of the spoon, disperse the last ⅓ cupful of solution over the surface of the soymilk; then gently, slowly stir the top half inch of the soymilk for about 15 seconds, cover the pot and wait for another 3 minutes (6 minutes if using Epsom salts).

Ladling the finished curds and whey into the 'settling box'.

11. Uncover the pot and stir contents to be sure that they have all separated into curds and whey. If there is still some milk left, stir it and cover the pot and leave it for a few more minutes, and if there is still milk left after that, add a little more curdling agent dissolved in water. (These last two steps should be unnecessary).

12. Dampen the muslin and use it to line the inside of your settling box, draping the extra length over the sides. Set the box over a pan or on a sink draining-board. I keep the whey, so I set the box on a rack over a pot large enough to collect the amount of whey that is released.

13. Place the cooking pot in the sink next to the settling box, and using the ladle or measuring cup, ladle the curds and whey from the cooking pot into the settling box. The curds will be held in the box, and the whey will flow out into the pot below.

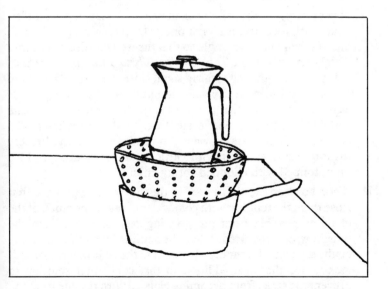

The tofu curds wrapped in a muslin cloth, covered by a weighted plate.

14. When the cooking pot is empty, fill it with cold water to assist cleaning. Fold the edges of the cloth over the curds in the settling box, so that the tofu curds are wrapped up like a package and the muslin cloth is covering everything. Place the lid on the box, set a weight (I use a jar filled with raisins or nuts) on the lid and press the curds for about 15 minutes. The longer the pressing, the firmer the tofu.

15. Fill the sink with cold water. Remove the weight and submerge the settling box in cold water. Remove the top of the box and invert it so that the wrapped tofu falls carefully out of the box and into the water in the sink.

16. Remove the box. Unwrap the tofu by letting its own weight pull it away from the muslin wrapping as you slowly and carefully lift the cloth out of the sink. (Be careful not to pull the muslin too sharply or it will pull away with some tofu attached.) The tofu cake will settle slowly to the bottom of the sink.

17. If necessary, cut the tofu block in half, and using a plate underneath each piece of tofu for support, lift pieces out of the water and set the plate at an angle so that the tofu can drain. I always weigh it at this stage. *Tofu is now ready to eat or use in cooking.*

   If you are not using it fairly soon, store the tofu in a covered container submerged in water and put it into the refrigerator or a cool place. Remember that freshly made tofu is more delicate and will break apart more easily than it will after it has cooled completely in its soaking water, so handle it carefully. Freshly made tofu is lovely eaten with a little natural soy sauce sprinkled on it, topped with chopped spring onions.

18. *Note:* To clean the cloths used in the tofu making process, first rinse them thoroughly with cold water to release as much of the okara as possible from the pressing sack and tofu from the muslin which you used to line the settling boxes. Then let the cloths soak for a few hours overnight in the cold water. I am still looking for the ideal addition to that cold water solution to prevent the sacks from becoming clogged with residue from the soymilk. I have been able to clean out cloths which have become

so clogged that the soymilk doesn't go through effectively when I press and squeeze the sack to separate the milk from the okara. I have cleaned them by soaking them in a bleach solution for a day or more, but the bleach solution tends to weaken the fabric causing it to burst easily under the pressure of squeezing out the milk. I think that there may be a product used in the dairy industry (perhaps for cheese making equipment), which would actually 'eat' the protein which gets stuck in the cloths. Alternatively, I must be prepared to make new sacks when the old ones get so clogged that they become useless. After I have soaked the cloths in cold water for a while, I then put them through the usual household laundry process.

Although it is the pressing sack which becomes clogged (I never have any trouble with the muslin), the muslin cloths must also be cleaned thoroughly.

Regular, Firm and Silken Tofu

Regular tofu is just as it is as it comes out of the home or commercial manufacturing process. It holds together well, but it is still soft. Firm tofu is more concentrated, more compact, more solid, and it retains its shape well for frying or cutting up into cubes or any desired shape. There are several ways of making tofu more firm. If you are using calcium sulphate as a coagulant, you can simply use more of this to make a firmer tofu. If you are using nigari, more stirring makes a firmer tofu. In each case, longer pressing makes a firmer tofu as well. After it is made, you can make it still firmer by pressing and other methods described in the following pages.

Silken tofu is made from rich soymilk (that means there is less water relative to beans, so the milk is thicker), and half the amount of coagulant. After the coagulant is added, the curds and whey are kept together, poured into a bowl and left to cool. The curds are not separated from the whey. The silken tofu is not as firm as regular tofu, but it can be pressed to make it more firm, and it lends itself beautifully to puddings, blended dishes and such things. If you want to fry it, you can do so by slicing it first and then letting it stand for 10-15 minutes between two towels to reduce the moisture and give a firmer product.

Storing Tofu

Tofu must always be stored covered with water, otherwise it would develop a thick skin on it which would be most unpleasant. In the following pages, you will see that in some instances it is advisable to store it in the refrigerator out of water for no more than 12 hours, but that for any longer period it must be kept in water. The water must be changed every day. It should keep for about a week in this way if it is kept quite cool in the refrigerator. I have kept it for about 10 days, but when it is 10 days old, I would use it only for frying and not for blending in any recipe or for using in salads. Alternatively, if I thought that I wouldn't use the tofu that I had, I would freeze it.

Keeping Tofu Fresh

Naturally, the fresher the tofu, the better it is, as with most foods. Of course, when you are able to buy tofu locally, it will be quite easy to buy according to your needs, so that you won't have the problem of having to keep it for too long. Also, when you are making it at home, you can generally judge your needs fairly accurately, but there are always times when the unexpected happens, and you find that you have tofu which has been kept for too long. I have successfully frozen old tofu and used it later with no ill effects, and if it is not too sour, I have fried it with no problem. If it is just sour, it may be parboiled to remove the sour odour and flavour; it may be deep-fried with the same result; or it may be used in something that requires a sour flavour, as one might use sour cream — perhaps cooked in a sauce, maybe blended first. If it has begun to smell bad and if it is slimy to the touch and shows signs of mould growth, it is really no good for use anymore.

Possible Problems in Tofu Making

I usually reckon to get about twice the weight in tofu that I use in dry beans. If I am able to get the larger soybeans that are specifically for tofu-soymilk making, the yield is better.

If, on the other hand, you have a low yield, you may be using old soybeans that don't release the milk as easily as fresh ones. If your beans are older than one year, don't use them for tofu making unless you have no alternative. If you have not soaked the beans long enough, you will also get a low yield — check again under the directions for soaking the beans. Make sure that the pressing sack is not too tightly woven, thus preventing the milk from going through. Also, if you add the curdling agent too quickly or put too much of it in, you might get a low yield. As far as measuring the curdling agent goes, this is clearly not a case for which the policy of 'if a little is good, a lot is better' works; quite the opposite. Too much curdling agent reduces the yield.

If tofu is not firm enough, you may have added too much curdling agent too quickly, or not stirred the curdling agent sufficiently. Be sure to stir it gently but for sufficient time. If you find that the curds are not separating from the whey, you may have used too little curdling agent, or you may have allowed the milk to cool too much before adding the agent.

Commercially Produced Tofu
Ordinary tofu which is produced for a soy delicatessen or Chinese restaurant must be treated just like home-produced tofu as in the section on storing tofu. This tofu may be commercially produced, but it is not packaged in such a way as to increase its shelf life, so it requires no further instructions than those for home-produced tofu.

Vacuum-packed Commercially Produced Tofu
If it is not already available in your area, the time will come when you will be able to buy vacuum-packed tofu which is produced commercially. This tofu will keep for 3 weeks to a month in its original container as long as the container is unopened. Once the package is opened, the tofu must be treated like freshly made tofu; the water should be changed daily, making sure that the tofu is well covered with water, and it must be refrigerated.

Silken Tofu in a Tetrapak Container
Silken tofu in the 'tetrapak' will keep for up to six months without refrigeration. After opening, it must be refrigerated and used within two days. It is free of preservatives, and it is packed in a way which

locks out air and germs which would spoil it. It is very convenient for everyone to have on hand since it doesn't require refrigeration, and it is especially useful in warm climates where refrigeration is not available. Naturally, it is also ideal for camping or hiking.

Where to Buy Tofu
Try health food stores, natural food sections of supermarkets, or refrigerator cases in supermarkets, Chinese shops or restaurants as sources of tofu.

Instructions for Making Tofu from Soy Flour
I feel that I must now mention the possibility of making tofu from soy flour. It is certainly possible to do this, and I include a simple recipe which I have adapted from several others. I include this recipe for those of you who don't at this moment have a blender/ liquidizer and would like to have some idea of what tofu is like before you purchase one, but I do want to say that I feel that I would prefer tofu made from whole soybeans. You will need the same equipment that is needed for making tofu with beans except for the blender.

First set out the equipment.
1. To 1 lb (½ kilo or 4 cupsful) of soy flour, add 3 quarts (3 litres) of warm water. It is necessary to add only a small amount of water to the flour first, and to mix the flour well into a smooth paste before adding it to the rest of the water. This avoids lumps in the mixture.
2. Let the water/soy flour mixture soak for at least half an hour. Stir it from time to time during the soaking time to prevent lumps from forming.
3. After soaking, pour the liquid into the calico bag set into the colander and pressing pot, and expel as much soymilk as possible.
4. Add another 1 pint (½ litre or 2½ cupsful) of warm water. Again squeeze as much milk out of the bag as possible.
5. Put all the milk into the cooking pot and bring it to the boil

carefully, reducing the heat after the milk has boiled.

6. Use about 1½ teaspoonsful of nigari or ¼ cupful of cider vinegar in 1 cupful of water, and stir well to dissolve it. Stir the milk and pour in half of the solution. If, after a few minutes, the milk hasn't formed into curds and whey, stir in more of the solution.

7. Simmer for 20 minutes.

8. Pour the curds and whey into the muslin-lined settling box and press it according to the instructions beginning from no. 12 in the original instructions for tofu making (page 31). Follow the instructions from 12-17 to finish off the process.

Before going on to recipes in this section, I think that it is most important to describe the various ways of preparing tofu and of changing its consistency because it will help you to find a variety of ways to use tofu, and you will learn how to create the texture you want for any particular recipe idea.

Blending. Tofu may be blended in a liquidizer/blender. If there is some other liquid in the recipe, put that into the blender first, and add the tofu in small pieces. If it is tofu on its own with other ingredients that are not liquid, try putting the tofu in little by little; it may be necessary to add a little soymilk or water or dairy milk to help it along.

Parboiling. This method is used for several purposes: simply to heat up tofu if you are using it on its own or with a sauce or soy sauce; to make tofu more firm; and to freshen tofu that is starting to go sour. Bring enough water to the boil to cover the tofu (about 2 pints/1 litre per ½-¾ lb/225-350g of tofu). Put the tofu in the pot, cover it and bring the water back to the boil, then remove the pot from the heat and leave it for a few minutes until the tofu is thoroughly warmed. If you want to make the tofu firmer, cut it into smaller pieces before dropping it into the water. You can add about ½ teaspoonful of sea salt per ¾ lb (350g) of tofu or a stick of kombu (seaweed) if you want the tofu to be a little firmer and to have a salty flavour. The salt would be important if you were putting the tofu into a soup because it would prevent the tofu from changing texture as a result of a longer period of boiling.

Once tofu is parboiled, it should be used right away, and it isn't very suitable for blending. Parboiling causes a slight loss of flavour, so it is not to be recommended unless necessary.

Draining. This technique is used to make tofu more firm and to preserve its subtle flavour which is gradually lost in the water. Tofu may be drained by placing it on a clean, folded towel in a container, covering and leaving it in the refrigerator for no more than 12 hours. It can be placed on a plate which is slanted to allow water to run off; this can be done while working on other parts of a meal, so that it drains for about half an hour or an hour. It can also be placed in a colander in a bowl, and covered and left in the refrigerator — never for more than 12 hours out of water. If the tofu comes in a sealed plastic tub — the commercial variety — you just poke a hole in the bottom of the tub, let the water out and leave tofu in the tub, either in a colander or on a folded towel in a container as above. Drained tofu is good for crumbling into recipes such as the Eggless Egg Salad (page 76) or for cutting into cubes and using in any kind of salad, or for slicing or mashing or making into burgers.

Pressing. Pressing is used to make tofu firmer; light pressing makes it hold together a bit better for salads, but more importantly, longer pressing gives a really firm product that can be held up by one corner without breaking, and this is especially nice for deep frying, pan frying — in fact any kind of cooking in which you want the tofu to retain its shape without breaking or crumbling will benefit from this.

When pressing, you can either leave the cake of tofu whole or slice it; the slices should be of uniform thickness so that it will press evenly. Then put the slices down on a layer of one or two absorbent towels, cover with more towels, then put a cutting board or biscuit tin on top of it and put a weight of about 4-5 lb (2-2½ kilos) on top. This can be left for an hour or two or overnight in the refrigerator if you want a really sturdy piece or pieces of tofu. The towels can be changed frequently, as they get wet from the draining water, and this will speed up the pressing; alternatively, the whole arrangement can be put on a slanted board (towards the sink) to allow the draining water to run off more easily.

Squeezing. Tofu can be squeezed after draining, pressing or parboiling, but you needn't do those things first. Its purpose is to reduce the moisture content without losing the form for cottage cheese-type dishes. Simply put the tofu into the middle of a dry tea-towel (or tofu pressing sack), gather the towel around the tofu and twist it to close. Squeeze the 'sack' gently so as not to push the tofu itself through the sack. Squeeze it this way or knead it for several minutes to get rid of some of the liquid content.

Scrambling. This method allows more liquid to be expelled than the squeezing method, and this yields firmer, more crumbly curds. Put the tofu into an unheated, dry pan and break it into pieces with a spatula or large spoon. Cook it over a medium heat for about 5 minutes, meanwhile stirring and continuing to break up the tofu. When whey separates from the curds, pour the contents of the pan into a fine strainer and let it drain for about half a minute if you want soft curds and for about 3 minutes if you want firmer curds. Spread the curds on a plate or cutting board to cool.

Reshaping. This technique produces a product which is very firm and which holds together well — something like a slice of cheese or meat. This is for any dish when one needs the tofu to have such a consistency and to hold its shape well when mixed into a casserole or salad. To about 2 lb (1 kilo) or 4 cupsful of tofu, add 1 teaspoonful of sea salt or 1 tablespoonful of natural soy sauce (or to taste). Cook it in a pan over a medium heat until the tofu is boiling vigorously. Remove the tofu from the pan and drain it in a cloth-lined colander for a few minutes. Then wrap the cloth carefully around the tofu and shape it into a piece about one inch thick. Put it onto a cutting board, making sure to slant the cutting board allowing for drainage. Press it in this way with a very heavy weight — for example, an 8 pint pot filled with water — and leave it to drain in a cool place for a couple of hours.

Crumbling. To 10 oz (300g) or 1¼ cupsful of tofu, add about ⅓ pint (200ml) of water and bring it to a boil while breaking up the tofu. Then lower the heat and simmer it for a couple of minutes. Pour the contents of a pan into cloth-lined colander, twist the cloth around the tofu and press it with a jar or the back of a serving spoon to get rid of as much liquid as possible. Then put the tofu into a bowl and break up more if you want smaller pieces for the dish you are preparing. This method is good for sauces, salads (in particular, Eggless Egg Salad, page 76).

This 'crumbling method' might also be used as the beginning stage of a reshaping process; after the liquid is expelled from the tofu, it can be shaped into a thickness of about one inch covered with a cloth, placed on a slanted cutting board and left under a pot filled with about 4 pints (2 litres) or 10 cupsful of water for an hour or two in a cool place. (One further way to achieve a crumbled texture is to put the tofu through a hand mill or meat grinder.)

After you have decided on the consistency of the tofu that you require for the particular recipe, you may go ahead and use any cooking method that is suitable. I might add that you can get on quite happily without using these methods each time you use tofu in cooking, but it is nice to know that they are possible because then one can get some idea of the versatility of the food.

Freezing Tofu. If you have too much tofu, don't hesitate to freeze it, but don't expect it to come out of the freezer looking and feeling the same as it did when you put it in! When tofu is frozen, it changes to a tan colour, and it looks very much like a sponge. When it is defrosted, it can be used in spaghetti sauces and stews, and recipes in which a 'meat-like' texture is required. After defrosting it, you must squeeze out as much liquid as possible by wrapping it in a clean tea-towel and putting it into a colander with a weight on top of it for about 15-30 minutes, or just take the cloth and squeeze the water out if you haven't time to wait for it to drain. If you want to defrost it in a hurry, put it into a bowl with hot water in it (left in its plastic bag in which it was frozen), and that will speed up the process.

Add the defrosted tofu to any recipe that you wish. It will absorb flavours beautifully and will become a nice chewy chunk of 'meat-lessness'. With its sponge-like consistency, you must remember that it soaks up flavourings like a sponge, and if you were to deep fry it, you would find that it would soak up a lot of oil. One way that I really enjoy it is simply defrosted and sliced, then sprinkled lightly with natural soy sauce and used between bread slices like a sandwich filling. You can also add slices of tomato, chopped onions, pieces of lettuce or any number of things that you fancy to this kind of sandwich.

Home-processed Soy Protein. You can make your own home-processed soy protein simply by sprinkling the pressed, defrosted tofu with soy sauce according to taste — about 1 tablespoonful to a ½ pint (¼ litre) by measure of the tofu. Make sure that the soy sauce is evenly distributed throughout. The HSP may be used as it is, or stored in the fridge for up to a week; or it may be dried in a slow oven — not over 250°F/130°C (Gas Mark ½) — and kept indefinitely once it is thoroughly dry in an airtight container. To rehydrate it, mix each cup of HSP with 1 cupful of water and set it aside for 20 minutes or add it as it is to soups and stews which have enough liquid in them to cause the HSP to rehydrate without any difficulty. There you have it — the basics of how to make and use tofu.

Note: Most recipes will serve 3-4 people.

2.

A WORD ABOUT THE RECIPES

I have included a selection of recipes which are to be used as guides and changed in any way that you would like. Everyone has different tastes, so that the flavouring or seasoning which I might enjoy might not suit you at all, so please be flexible, experimental and adventuresome in using the following recipes.

You will notice in most of the recipes that when vanilla is used, I usually give one measurement and then an alternative. I do this because different kinds of vanilla have very different strengths and distinct flavours. I assume that you will be used to using a particular brand of vanilla and that you will be able to determine what amount will best suit the recipe, but please be aware that different brands of vanilla must be treated differently.

One of my aims in my own cooking and in writing this book is to rid myself of the dependence on animal products, so I have not used eggs in many recipes and where they are included, I have usually given an alternative. There are several ways of using tofu as a substitute for eggs. Some people have suggested that about 4 oz (100g) of tofu (blended) is a good substitute for each egg, and others have said that 1 tablespoonful of tofu blended with 1 tablespoonful of water can make a good mixture to be used as a substitute with the recommendation that you take 1 tablespoonful of that mixture to replace each egg in the recipe. My suggestion is that both methods may be effective, and that they must be tried in recipes which call for eggs. Alternatively, if you are making croquettes, for instance, you can use extra flour and some soymilk in place of an egg. Just because I have not included eggs in most of the recipes doesn't mean that you are not free to add them when you like, but it should be useful for those who are allergic to eggs to have as many recipes as possible which are free of them.

As an example of how a recipe may be changed, I will show you one of my favourite recipes which calls for eggs and then show you the possible alternatives to using eggs.

This is my original recipe for carob brownies:

Imperial (Metric)	American
¾ cupful honey	1 cupful honey
¾ cupful vegetable oil	1 cupful vegetable oil
1 teaspoonful sea salt	1 teaspoonful sea salt
4 eggs, separated	4 eggs, separated
2 teaspoonsful pure vanilla essence	2 teaspoonsful pure vanilla essence
1 cupful wholewheat flour	1⅓ cupsful wholewheat flour
½ cupful carob powder	⅔ cupful carob powder

1. Combine the honey and oil either by hand or in an electric mixer until they are well blended.

2. Add the salt, egg yolks, flour and carob powder and beat them well.

3. Fold in the stiffly beaten egg whites and pour the mixture into an oiled cake tin and bake at 325°F/170°C (Gas Mark 3) for about 35 minutes.

Note: In order to eliminate eggs in the recipe, you might substitute 1 lb (½ kilo) of tofu which has been blended until it is smooth, or you might use 4 oz (100g) of tofu blended with ½ cupful of water to replace the 4 eggs. If you simply want to cut down on eggs rather than eliminate them entirely, you could use 1 or 2 eggs and sub- stitute tofu for the others. It really depends on your requirements and on what your eating habits are. With or without the eggs, if you want the brownies to rise more, you could add 2 teaspoonsful of baking powder. Another alternative to the use of eggs in baking cakes is shown in the cake recipes using okara.

I use honey and/or dried fruit for sweetening. I have chosen not to use white or brown sugar for many reasons. I use freshly ground wholewheat flour in my cooking. I have a wonderful electric grain mill by *Samap* which I have been using for years to grind whole wheat grains into fine wholewheat flour as I need it. I prefer to use a good quality vegetable oil from the natural food store instead of butter or margarine in my cooking for most recipes. I do use some sea salt or biochemic salt, but more and more people are cutting down or eliminating salt from their diets, so it is wise to be aware of how much salt you are using in all your cooking.

Take heart and take note! When I began writing this book, I thought that it would be wonderful if there were a tofu kit available in this country which I could recommend in the book. I asked a number of people about such a possibility and received very little response, so I dropped the whole idea. Then all of a sudden, I found myself talking to someone who was interested! At the time of writing, there is a prototype of a tofu maker being constructed which I will test and use and for which I will offer suggestions for alterations, if necessary. Not only is there a possibility of a tofu making unit, but also the hope of a tempeh maker, as well. So watch for news of these things from *Ambig Products Ltd*, London SW13; these are the people who already make sprouters.

3.
RECIPES

FRIED TOFU

Tofu may be cut into slices, cubes or fingers, marinated first in natural soy sauce with possible additions of such things as ginger, garlic, honey and vinegar (for sweet and sour) or tomato sauce; it may even be used on its own.

The tofu may then be dipped in wholewheat flour or not, as you wish, and either shallow fried or deep fried according to your taste. This makes a lovely main meat substitute dish.

CURRIED NOODLES WITH DEEP FRIED TOFU

Imperial (Metric)	American
2 tablespoonsful vegetable oil	2 tablespoonsful vegetable oil
2 carrots, cut into matchstick pieces	2 carrots, cut into matchstick pieces
1 large onion, sliced	1 large onion, sliced
3 oz (75g) raisins	½ cupful raisins
2 sticks celery, chopped	2 sticks celery, chopped
1 apple, diced	1 apple, diced
4 tablespoonsful water	¼ cupful water
1 tablespoonful curry powder	1 tablespoonful curry powder
1 teaspoonful sea salt	1 teaspoonful sea salt
1 tablespoonful natural soy sauce	1 tablespoonful natural soy sauce
1 lb (½ kilo) deep fried tofu cubes (page 45)	2 cupsful deep fried tofu cubes (page 45)
½ lb (¼ kilo) buckwheat or wholewheat noodles, cooked	½ lb buckwheat or wholewheat noodles, cooked

1. *Sauté* the carrots in the oil for a couple of minutes, add the onions and cook them for a few minutes.

2. Add the raisins, celery and apple and stir fry them for a few more minutes.

3. Stir in the water, curry powder, salt, soy sauce and deep fried tofu cubes.

4. Add the cooked noodles and serve.

FRUIT AND NUT CASSEROLE

Imperial (Metric)	**American**
1 large onion, thinly sliced	1 large onion, thinly sliced
2 cloves garlic, crushed	2 cloves garlic, crushed
2½ tablespoonsful vegetable oil	3 tablespoonsful vegetable oil
⅓ pint (200ml) water	1 cupful water
2½ tablespoonsful natural soy sauce	3 tablespoonsful natural soy sauce
1 tablespoonful treacle, light molasses or honey	1 tablespoonful treacle, light molasses or honey
2 tablespoonsful peanut butter	2 tablespoonsful peanut butter
¼ teaspoonful ground cardamom	¼ teaspoonful ground cardamom
¼ teaspoonful grated nutmeg	¼ teaspoonful grated nutmeg
3 oz (75g) raisins	½ cupful raisins
2 oz (50g) cashew nuts, lightly toasted	½ cupful cashew nuts, lightly toasted
1 lb (½ kilo) tofu, diced into ¼ inch cubes	2 cupsful tofu, diced into ¼ inch cubes
2 bananas, chopped into ½ inch pieces	2 bananas, chopped into ½ inch pieces

1. *Sauté* the onion and garlic in the oil for a few minutes, then add everything else except for the tofu and bananas.

2. Stir the mixture well until the peanut butter is blended in.

3. Add the diced tofu and banana pieces. Simmer the casserole for 5-10 minutes and serve over cooked brown rice.

TOFU SPINACH QUICHE

Pastry

Imperial (Metric)	American
1 lb (½ kilo) wholewheat flour	4 cupsful wholewheat flour
4½ tablespoonsful vegetable oil	6 tablespoonsful vegetable oil
Pinch of sea salt	Pinch of sea salt
A little cold water	A little cold water

1. Combine the ingredients, and knead the dough into a cohesive ball.

2. Roll out the pastry on a floured board and press it into a greased pie dish.

Filling

Imperial (Metric)	American
2 onions, diced	2 onions, diced
¼ pint (150ml) vegetable oil	¾ cupful vegetable oil
2 tablespoonsful chopped parsley	2 tablespoonsful chopped parsley
2 tablespoonsful dill weed	2 tablespoonsful dill weed
1½ cupsful chopped and cooked spinach or	2 cupsful chopped and cooked spinach or
2 (10 oz) packets frozen spinach	2 (10 oz) packets frozen spinach
Sea salt to taste	Sea salt to taste
1 lb (½ kilo) tofu	2 cupsful tofu
4 tablespoonsful soymilk (if necessary)	¼ cupful soymilk (if necessary)

1. *Sauté* the onions in oil until they are transparent.

2. Add the dill weed, parsley, spinach (defrosted) and salt and mix them in well.

3. Blend the tofu in a liquidizer with the soymilk if it is difficult to blend on its own. (You might also put the parsley into the blender to chop it up more easily.)

4. Pour this over the vegetable mixture and mix it thoroughly.

5. Place the filling in the pastry case and bake it at 375°F/190°C (Gas Mark 5) for about 30 minutes.

TOFU BURGERS

Imperial (Metric)	American
2 lb (1 kilo) tofu	4 cupsful tofu
4½ tablespoonsful grated carrot	6 tablespoonsful grated carrot
1 small onion or several spring onions, finely chopped	1 small onion or several scallions, finely chopped
2 tablespoonsful sunflower seeds	2 tablespoonsful sunflower seeds
1 teaspoonful sea salt	1 teaspoonful sea salt
2 tablespoonsful raisins	2 tablespoonsful raisins
Vegetable oil for deep frying	Vegetable oil for deep frying

1. Drain the tofu between two layers of clean tea-towels and press it down with a weight for about half an hour.

2. Place the tofu in a bowl and knead it for a few minutes.

3. Add the remaining ingredients and knead them together for a few minutes until well mixed.

4. Shape the mixture into burgers and deep fry them for a few minutes until done.

SPAGHETTI SAUCE

Imperial (Metric)	American
1 large onion, chopped	1 large onion, chopped
4 large cloves garlic, minced	4 large cloves garlic, minced
2 tablespoonsful vegetable oil	2 tablespoonsful vegetable oil
1 lb (½ kilo) tofu, mashed well with a fork or leftover scrambled tofu	2 cupsful tofu, mashed well with a fork or leftover scrambled tofu
2 medium-sized tins tomatoes or 2 lb (1 kilo) fresh tomatoes	2 medium-sized tins tomatoes or 2 lb fresh tomatoes
1 small tin tomato paste	1 small tin tomato paste
½ tablespoonful oregano	½ tablespoonful oregano
½ tablespoonful basil	½ tablespoonful basil
½ tablespoonful thyme	½ tablespoonful thyme
2 oz (50g) mushrooms, sliced	1 cupful mushrooms, sliced
Natural soy sauce to taste	Natural soy sauce to taste

1. *Sauté* the onion and garlic in the oil and then add the other ingredients.

2. Bring the mixture to the boil, reduce the heat and simmer the sauce for about half an hour. Serve over wholewheat or buckwheat spaghetti.

EGGLESS TOFU SCRAMBLED EGGS

Imperial (Metric)	American
2 onions, chopped	2 onions, chopped
2 tablespoonsful vegetable oil	2 tablespoonsful vegetable oil
1 lb (½ kilo) tofu, mashed with a fork	2 cupsful tofu, mashed with a fork
1 tablespoonful natural soy sauce (or to taste)	1 tablespoonful natural soy sauce (or to taste)
½ teaspoonful turmeric	½ teaspoonful turmeric

1. *Sauté* the onions in the oil until they are transparent.

2. Add the mashed tofu, soy sauce and turmeric and continue to cook until the tofu is nicely browned.

MARINATED TOFU STEAKS FOR BAKING

Imperial (Metric)	American
1½ lb (¾ kilo) tofu, cut into half inch pieces	3 cupsful tofu, cut into half inch pieces
⅓ pint (200ml) natural soy sauce	1 cupful natural soy sauce
2 cloves garlic, minced	2 cloves garlic, minced
1 tablespoonful vegetable oil	1 tablespoonful vegetable oil
2 tablespoonsful honey	2 tablespoonsful honey
2½ tablespoonsful cider vinegar	3 tablespoonsful cider vinegar

1. Marinate the tofu in the remaining ingredients for 1-4 hours, turning it occasionally.

2. Bake the pieces on a greased baking sheet at 400°F/200°C (Gas Mark 6). Turn the pieces over once.

TOFU TAMALE PIE

Imperial (Metric)	American
2 onions, chopped	2 onions, chopped
2 green peppers, chopped	2 green peppers, chopped
3 cloves garlic, minced	3 cloves garlic, minced
3 tablespoonsful vegetable oil	4 tablespoonsful vegetable oil
1½ lb (¾ kilo) tofu	3 cupsful tofu
2 lb (1 kilo) tomatoes, fresh or tinned	2 lb tomatoes, fresh or tinned
1½ cupsful sweet corn	2 cupsful sweet corn
⅓ pint (200ml) water	1 cupful water
2 tablespoonsful chilli powder	2 tablespoonsful chilli powder
2 tablespoonsful natural soy sauce (or to taste)	2 tablespoonsful natural soy sauce (or to taste)
1 teaspoonful cumin	1 teaspoonful cumin
¾ cupful corn meal	1 cupful corn meal

1. *Sauté* the onions, peppers and garlic in the oil, using a large ovenproof casserole.

2. Add the remaining ingredients, place the casserole in the oven and bake it at 350°F/180°C (Gas Mark 4) for about 1 hour. (If desired, put sliced cheese on top, although this dish is good without as well.)

SHALLOW FRIED TOFU STEAKS

Imperial (Metric)
Tofu slices about ⅓ inch thick
Natural soy sauce
Wholewheat flour (optional)
Vegetable oil

American
Tofu slices about ⅓ inch thick
Natural soy sauce
Wholewheat flour (optional)
Vegetable oil

1. Leave the tofu slices in the soy sauce for a couple of minutes, then turn them and leave them again for another couple of minutes.

2. Dip them in the flour; this will give a crispy coating.

3. Fry the pieces of tofu in the oil for a few minutes on each side until they are nicely browned. Serve with vegetables and a salad.

TOFU CHILLI

Imperial (Metric)	**American**
1 large onion, chopped	1 large onion, chopped
2 cloves garlic, minced	2 cloves garlic, minced
2½ tablespoonsful vegetable oil	3 tablespoonsful vegetable oil
2 medium-sized tins tomatoes or	2 medium-sized tins tomatoes or
2 lb (1 kilo) fresh tomatoes, cut up	2 lb fresh tomatoes, cut up
3 cupsful kidney or pinto beans	4 cupsful kidney or pinto beans
1 tablespoonful chilli powder	1 tablespoonful chilli powder
1 teaspoonful cumin	1 teaspoonful cumin
1 teaspoonful sea salt (or to taste) or	1 teaspoonful sea salt (or to taste) or
1 tablespoonful natural soy sauce (or to taste)	1 tablespoonful natural soy sauce (or to taste)
1 bay leaf	1 bay leaf
2 lb (1 kilo) frozen tofu, thawed, squeezed dry and crumbled	4 cupsful frozen tofu, thawed, squeezed dry and crumbled

1. *Sauté* the onion and garlic in the oil until the onion is transparent.

2. Add the remaining ingredients, bring to the boil and simmer covered for 1 hour.

RANCHO CASSEROLE

Imperial (Metric)	American
2 large onions, chopped	2 large onions, chopped
4 sticks of celery, chopped	4 sticks of celery, chopped
6 medium-sized potatoes, chopped	6 medium-sized potatoes, chopped
2½ tablespoonsful vegetable oil	3 tablespoonsful vegetable oil
8 tomatoes, chopped	8 tomatoes, chopped
1 small tin tomato paste	1 small tin tomato paste
2 lb (1 kilo) frozen tofu	4 cupsful frozen tofu
2½ tablespoonsful natural soy sauce	3 tablespoonsful natural soy sauce

1. *Sauté* the onions, celery and potatoes in the oil.

2. Add the tomatoes and tomato paste and continue to cook.

3. Add the frozen tofu and break it up in the casserole.

4. Add the soy sauce and cook until the vegetables are done, adding more water if necessary. (Extra water should not be necessary because of the liquid in the tomatoes especially.)

ITALIAN STYLE MEATLESS MEATBALLS

Imperial (Metric)	American
1 lb (½ kilo) tofu, well broken up	2 cupsful tofu, well broken up
either:	either:
2 eggs, lightly beaten and	2 eggs, lightly beaten and
1 oz (25g) wholewheat breadcrumbs	½ cupful wholewheat breadcrumbs
or:	or:
4 oz (100g) wholewheat flour and	1 cupful wholewheat flour and
2 oz (50g) wholewheat breadcrumbs	1 cupful wholewheat breadcrumbs
1 teaspoonful oregano	1 teaspoonful oregano
½ teaspoonful basil	½ teaspoonful basil
1 small onion, finely chopped	1 small onion, finely chopped
1 tablespoonful natural soy sauce	1 tablespoonful natural soy sauce
(or to taste)	(or to taste)

1. Combine the ingredients well in a large bowl, kneading the mixture a little to help it hold together.

2. Shape the mixture into balls and shallow fry or deep fry them. Use these with spaghetti or bake them in the oven with a nice Italian style tomato sauce (page 50).

3. Bake at 350°F/180°C (Gas Mark 4) for about half an hour.

DEEP FRIED TOFU IN BREADCRUMB BATTER

Imperial (Metric)	American
1 lb (½ kilo) tofu	2 cupsful tofu
3 tablespoonsful natural soy sauce	4 tablespoonsful natural soy sauce
4 oz (100g) wholewheat flour	1 cupful wholewheat flour
either:	either:
1 egg	1 egg
or:	or:
4 oz (100g) wholewheat flour and	1 cupful wholewheat flour and
⅓ pint (200ml) water	1 cupful water
Wholewheat breadcrumbs	Wholewheat breadcrumbs
Vegetable oil for frying	Vegetable oil for frying

1. If necessary, press the tofu to make it firm enough to hold together, then cut it into fingers or slices.

2. Dip the pieces of tofu in the soy sauce, turn them and leave them for a few minutes to marinate.

3. Remove the tofu and dip it in the wholewheat flour, covering all sides of each piece.

4. Dip the tofu in the egg or flour and water mixture (this is lovely) and finally dip it in the breadcrumbs, making sure that all sides are well covered.

5. Drop the pieces in hot oil and deep fry them for 3-4 minutes until brown. (If you like, these can be shallow fried by using a generous amount of oil in the pan and turning them once to cook both sides.)

Note: Home-made breadcrumbs are best if dried for about half an hour in the oven at the lowest setting. They can be made in this way and kept in a fridge for a long time to be used whenever breadcrumbs are called for.

TOFU FRENCH TOAST WITHOUT EGGS

Imperial (Metric)	American
½ lb (¼ kilo) tofu	1 cupful tofu
1 tablespoonful honey (optional)	1 tablespoonful honey (optional)
4 tablespoonsful water	¼ cupful water
2 teaspoonsful natural soy sauce	2 teaspoonsful natural soy sauce
4-6 slices of wholewheat bread	4-6 slices of wholewheat bread

1. Blend the tofu, honey (if used), water and soy sauce until smooth.

2. Dip both sides of the bread in the batter and fry each piece in vegetable oil until done, turning it once. Serve with honey, apple sauce or jam, or the American favourite — maple syrup.

Variation
Add some honey to the Tofu Mayonnaise (page 62) and dip the slices of bread into it before frying them in vegetable oil.

SCRAMBLED TOFU

Mash some tofu with a fork and fry it in a little vegetable oil. Add tamari (natural soy sauce) to taste whilst frying. The addition of a little turmeric will make this look like scrambled eggs.

TOFU GUACAMOLE

Imperial (Metric)	American
1 ripe avocado	1 ripe avocado
1½ lb (¾ kilo) tofu	3 cupsful tofu
3 tablespoonsful vegetable oil or mayonnaise	4 tablespoonsful vegetable oil or mayonnaise
2 teaspoonsful sea salt	2 teaspoonsful sea salt
2 tablespoonsful lemon juice	2 tablespoonsful lemon juice
1 onion, chopped	1 onion, chopped

1. Blend all the ingredients, adjusting the flavourings to suit your own taste. Use this as a dip for raw vegetable pieces or potato crisps, or as a salad dressing.

MISO TOFU DRESSING

Imperial (Metric)	American
¾ lb (350g) tofu	1½ cupsful tofu
4 tablespoonsful soymilk	¼ cupful soymilk
2½ tablespoonsful vegetable oil	3 tablespoonsful vegetable oil
4 tablespoonsful lemon juice	¼ cupful lemon juice
2 tablespoonsful miso (or to taste)	2 tablespoonsful miso (or to taste)

1. Blend all the ingredients until smooth.

TAHINI TOFU SALAD DRESSING

Imperial (Metric)	American
3 tablespoonsful tahini	4 tablespoonsful tahini
½ lb (¼ kilo) tofu	1 cupful tofu
2 tablespoonsful vegetable oil	2 tablespoonsful vegetable oil
1 clove garlic, chopped	1 clove garlic, chopped
Juice of 3 lemons (or to taste)	Juice of 3 lemons (or to taste)
½ teaspoonful sea salt	½ teaspoonful sea salt
4 tablespoonsful water (or as necessary)	¼ cupful water (or as necessary)

1. Blend all the ingredients well.

TANGY LEMON-HONEY DRESSING

Imperial (Metric)	American
1 lb (½ kilo) tofu	2 cupsful tofu
2 tablespoonsful vegetable oil	2 tablespoonsful vegetable oil
6 tablespoonsful lemon juice	⅓ cupful lemon juice
6 tablespoonsful honey	⅓ cupful honey
½ teaspoonful sea salt	½ teaspoonful sea salt
¼ teaspoonful dry mustard	¼ teaspoonful dry mustard
1 tablespoonful grated lemon rind	1 tablespoonful grated lemon rind

1. Blend all the ingredients well.

SILKEN LEMON-HONEY DRESSING

Imperial (Metric)	American
1 packet Morinaga silken tofu	1 packet Morinaga silken tofu
2 tablespoonsful lemon juice	2 tablespoonsful lemon juice
2 tablespoonsful honey	2 tablespoonsful honey
¼ teaspoonful sea salt	¼ teaspoonful sea salt
1 teaspoonful grated lemon rind	1 teaspoonful grated lemon rind

1. Blend all the ingredients well.

TOFU LEMON MAYONNAISE

Imperial (Metric)	American
¾ lb (350g) tofu	1½ cupsful tofu
4 tablespoonsful soymilk	¼ cupful soymilk
4 tablespoonsful lemon juice	¼ cupful lemon juice
2 tablespoonsful vegetable oil	2 tablespoonsful vegetable oil
½ teaspoonful sea salt	½ teaspoonful sea salt

1. Blend all the ingredients well. This dressing may be used as a mayonnaise substitute with potatoes, fish, grains, vegetables, etc.

MOCHA SURPRISE ICE CREAM
(Thanks to Darrilyn Jackson)

Imperial (Metric)	American
4 oz (100g) cashew nuts	1 cupful cashew nuts
1 pint (½ litre) water	2½ cupsful water
4 oz (100g) tofu	½ cupful tofu
½ lb (¼ kilo) honey	1 cupful honey
3 tablespoonsful carob powder	4 tablespoonsful carob powder
1 tablespoonful instant grain coffee (Swiss Cup or Barleycup)	1 tablespoonful instant grain coffee (Swiss Cup or Barleycup)
Pinch of sea salt	Pinch of sea salt
1½ teaspoonsful agar agar powder or 1 tablespoonful agar agar flakes	1½ teaspoonsful agar agar powder or 1 tablespoonful agar agar flakes
⅓ pint (200ml) soymilk	1 cupful soymilk
1½ teaspoonsful or a few drops pure vanilla essence	1½ teaspoonsful or a few drops pure vanilla essence
5 tablespoonsful vegetable oil	⅓ cupful vegetable oil

1. Dissolve the agar agar powder in the soymilk (or, if using flakes, soak them in the milk for 1 minute, boil them for 1 minute and leave them to cool for 1 minute).

2. Bring the milk to the boil, stirring constantly, and remove the pan from the heat immediately.

3. Grind the nuts to a powder, and add the water and soymilk.

4. Place all the ingredients in a liquidizer (except for the oil) and blend them until smooth. Taste for flavouring and sweetness.

5. Blend the mixture at high speed and add the oil slowly.

6. Place the mixture in an ice cream maker and follow the directions, or put it into a container in the freezer.

7. Remove the container and blend the mixture again before it freezes solid.

BANANA DESSERT

Imperial (Metric)
1 lb (½ kilo) tofu
1 or 2 ripe bananas
2 tablespoonsful honey
1 teaspoonful or a few drops pure
　vanilla essence
Pinch of sea salt

American
2 cupsful tofu
1 or 2 ripe bananas
2 tablespoonsful honey
1 teaspoonful or a few drops pure
　vanilla essence
Pinch of sea salt

1.　Blend all the ingredients well and serve chilled.

WHOLEWHEAT PASTRY CASE

Imperial (Metric)	American
1 lb (½ kilo) wholewheat flour	4 cupsful wholewheat flour
¼ teaspoonful sea salt	¼ teaspoonful sea salt
½ teaspoonful cinnamon	½ teaspoonful cinnamon
4 tablespoonsful vegetable oil	¼ cupful vegetable oil
2 tablespoonsful water	2 tablespoonsful water
2½ tablespoonsful honey	3 tablespoonsful honey

1. Combine the flour, salt, cinnamon and work in the oil, water and honey.

2. Press the pastry into a pie dish and bake for 10 minutes at 350°F/180°C (Gas Mark 4). Use this with any sweet filling.

CAROB BANANA CREAM PIE

Imperial (Metric)	American
1 lb (½ kilo) tofu	2 cupsful tofu
⅓ pint (200ml) soymilk	1 cupful soymilk
3 very ripe bananas	3 very ripe bananas
4 oz (100g) honey	½ cupful honey
1 teaspoonful or a few drops pure vanilla essence	1 teaspoonful or a few drops pure vanilla essence
4½ tablespoonsful carob powder	6 tablespoonsful carob powder
1½ teaspoonsful cinnamon	1½ teaspoonsful cinnamon
3 tablespoonsful agar agar flakes	4 tablespoonsful agar agar flakes

1. Blend the tofu, soymilk, bananas, honey, vanilla, carob and cinnamon.

2. Add the agar agar flakes dissolved in a little boiling water.

3. Pour the mixture into a wholewheat pastry case (page 65) and bake it at 350°F/180°C (Gas Mark 4) for about 45 minutes. Alternatively, bake the pastry case first, pour the mixture into it and leave it in the fridge for a few hours until set.

CAROB MINT PIE

Filling

Imperial (Metric)	American
1½ lb (¾ kilo) tofu	3 cupsful tofu
6 oz (150g) honey	¾ cupful honey
3 oz (75g) carob powder	¾ cupful carob powder
1 tablespoonful or a few drops pure vanilla essence (depending on type)	1 tablespoonful or a few drops pure vanilla essence (depending on type)
½ teaspoonful cinnamon	½ teaspoonful cinnamon
Pinch of sea salt	Pinch of sea salt
½ teaspoonful pure peppermint essence	½ teaspoonful pure pepermint essence

1. Blend all the ingredients in a liquidizer and pour the mixture into a wholewheat pastry case (page 65) or breadcrumb crust (below).

2. Bake at 425°F/220°C (Gas Mark 7) for about 45 minutes or until the crust is brown.

Breadcrumb Crust

Imperial (Metric)	American
4 oz (100g) wholewheat breadcrumbs (lightly toasted)	2 cupsful wholewheat breadcrumbs (lightly toasted)
1 teaspoonful cinnamon	1 teaspoonful cinnamon
2 tablespoonsful vegetable oil	2 tablespoonsful vegetable oil
2 tablespoonsful water	2 tablespoonsful water
2½ tablespoonsful honey	3 tablespoonsful honey

1. Combine the ingredients well and place the mixture in a greased pie dish.

2. Bake for 10 minutes at 350°F/180°C (Gas Mark 4) before adding the filling.

TOFU CREAM PIE

Imperial (Metric)	American
1 lb (½ kilo) tofu	2 cupsful tofu
4 tablespoonsful water	¼ cupful water
6 oz (150g) honey	¾ cupful honey
1 teaspoonful or a few drops pure vanilla essence	1 teaspoonful or a few drops pure vanilla essence
2½ tablespoonsful lemon juice	3 tablespoonsful lemon juice
2 teaspoonsful grated lemon rind	2 teaspoonsful grated lemon rind
¼ teaspoonful sea salt	¼ teaspoonful sea salt

1. Blend all the ingredients and pour the mixture into a prepared wholewheat pastry case (page 65) and bake at 350°F/180°C (Gas Mark 4) for 1 hour.

CAROB CAKE

Imperial (Metric)	American
½ lb (¼ kilo) honey	1 cupful honey
⅓ pint (200ml) vegetable oil	1 cupful vegetable oil
1 lb (½ kilo) tofu	2 cupsful tofu
1 teaspoonful pure vanilla essence	1 teaspoonful pure vanilla essence
10 oz (300g) wholewheat flour	2½ cupsful wholewheat flour
6 oz (150g) carob powder	1½ cupful carob powder
1 teaspoonful sea salt	1 teaspoonful sea salt

1. Blend the honey, oil, tofu, salt and vanilla.

2. Add the flour and carob and mix them well with a mixer or by hand.

3. Bake in a greased tin at 350°F/180°C (Gas Mark 4) for about 30 minutes.

PINEAPPLE CAKE

Imperial (Metric)	American
10 oz (300g) tofu	1¼ cupsful tofu
½ lb (¼ kilo) honey	1 cupful honey
4 tablespoonsful vegetable oil	¼ cupful vegetable oil
½ teaspoonful sea salt	½ teaspoonful sea salt
2 teaspoonsful baking powder	2 teaspoonsful baking powder
8 tablespoonsful soymilk	½ cupful soymilk
½ lb (¼ kilo) wholewheat flour	2 cupsful wholewheat flour
1 teaspoonful or a few drops pure vanilla essence (depending on type)	1 teaspoonful or a few drops pure vanilla essence (depending on type)
1 medium-sized tin pineapple in its own juice	1 medium-sized tin pineapple in its own juice
2 tablespoonsful honey	2 tablespoonsful honey
1 tablespoonful arrowroot	1 tablespoonful arrowroot

1. Blend the tofu, honey, oil, salt, baking powder, soymilk and vanilla.

2. Add the flour and place the mixture in a greased cake tin.

3. Arrange circles of pineapple on top on the cake mixture.

4. Make the topping by mixing together the honey and a little pineaple juice and bringing it to the boil.

5. Add the arrowroot which has already been stirred into a little pineapple juice until dissolved thoroughly, and simmer until the liquid becomes clear.

6. Pour this sauce over the pineapple slices and bake the cake at 375°F/190°C (Gas Mark 5) for about 20 minutes.

LEMON AND HONEY SAUCE

Imperial (Metric)	American
1 lb (½ kilo) tofu	2 cupsful tofu
3 tablespoonsful lemon juice	4 tablespoonsful lemon juice
3 tablespoonsful honey	4 tablespoonsful honey
¼ teaspoonful sea salt	¼ teaspoonful sea salt
1 tablespoonful grated lemon rind	1 tablespoonful grated lemon rind
4 tablespoonful soymilk	¼ cupful soymilk

1. Blend all the ingredients and serve.

Note: This is particularly good with vegetable salads.

WHIPPED CREAM TOFU

Imperial (Metric)	American
4 tablespoonsful water	¼ cupful water
¾ lb (350g) tofu	1½ cupsful tofu
½ teaspoonful pure vanilla essence	½ teaspoonful pure vanilla essence
½ teaspoonful sea salt	½ teaspoonful sea salt
2½ tablespoonsful vegetable oil	3 tablespoonsful vegetable oil
4 oz (100g) honey	½ cupful honey

1. Blend all the ingredients and adjust the flavouring to taste.

TOFU SMOOTHIE

Imperial (Metric)	American
Tofu	Tofu
Frozen fruit — bananas, peaches, nectarines, strawberries, etc.	Frozen fruit — bananas, peaches, nectarines, strawberries, etc.
Honey to taste	Honey to taste
Water or apple juice	Water or apple juice
Sesame tahini (optional)	Sesame tahini (optional)
Pure vanilla essence (optional)	Pure vanilla essence (optional)

1. Blend all the ingredients in a liquidizer.

2. Flavour to taste and serve as a milk shake.

CURRIED TOFU SPREAD

Imperial (Metric)	American
1 lb (½ kilo) very fresh tofu, mashed well with a fork	2 cupsful very fresh tofu, mashed well with a fork
2-4 tablespoonsful mayonnaise	2-4 tablespoonsful mayonnaise
1 teaspoonful curry powder	1 teaspoonful curry powder
1 tablespoonful natural soy sauce	1 tablespoonful natural soy sauce

1. Mix the ingredients well with a fork and serve the spread on biscuits, crackers or salad.

TOFU CHAPATTIS

Imperial (Metric)	American
1 lb (½ kilo) tofu	2 cupsful tofu
8 tablespoonsful vegetable oil	½ cupful vegetable oil
½ teaspoonful sea salt	½ teaspoonful sea salt
1 tablespoonful baking powder	1 tablespoonful baking powder
¾ lb (350g) wholewheat flour	3 cupsful wholewheat flour

1. Blend all the ingredients in a liquidizer.

2. Roll out the mixture into rounds, place them on a greased baking sheet and bake them at 350°F/180°C (Gas Mark 4) for about 12 minutes or until done.

MISO SOUP WITH TOFU CUBES

Imperial (Metric)
A little vegetable oil
1 onion, chopped
1 carrot, sliced
1 stick celery, sliced
2 pints (1 litre) water
1 piece seaweed (wakame), rinsed
 and soaked for about 10 minutes
 and finely chopped
½ lb (¼ kilo) tofu, pressed until firm
 and cut into cubes
1 tablespoonful miso (or to taste)

American
A little vegetable oil
1 onion, chopped
1 carrot, sliced
1 stick celery, sliced
5 cupsful water
1 piece seaweed (wakame), rinsed
 and soaked for about 10 minutes
 and finely chopped
1 cupful tofu, pressed until firm
 and cut into cubes
1 tablespoonful miso (or to taste)

1. Brush a little oil onto the base of a large pan and *sauté* the onion for a couple of minutes.

2. Add the carrot and celery and *sauté* them for a few more minutes.

3. Add the water and *wakame*, bring the soup to the boil and cook until the vegetables are done — about 20 minutes or so.

4. At the end of cooking, add the tofu cubes, bring the soup back to the boil briefly, then remove the pan from the heat and mix the miso with a small amount of soup stock to dissolve it.

5. Add this to the soup or put the miso into individual bowls and ladle the soup into the bowls; this way amounts of miso can be adjusted to each person's taste or needs.

TOFU SANDWICH FILLINGS

Imperial (Metric)
Frozen tofu
Natural soy sauce
Other flavourings, such as Ketchup,
   mustard, etc.

American
Frozen tofu
Natural soy sauce
Other flavourings, such as Ketchup,
   mustard, etc.

Thaw the frozen tofu, slice it and sprinkle the soy sauce lightly over it. This can be used in sandwiches and has a lovely flavour. Top with onions, slices of tomatoes and cheese if you wish, and experiment with all types of flavourings for fun.

EGGLESS EGG SALAD

Imperial (Metric)	**American**
1½ lb (¾ kilo) tofu, pressed for half an hour and mashed with a fork	3 cupsful tofu, pressed for half an hour and mashed with a fork
1 stick celery, finely chopped	1 stick celery, finely chopped
1 small onion or 3-4 spring onions, chopped	1 small onion or 3-4 scallions, chopped
1 tablespoonful natural soy sauce	1 tablespoonful natural soy sauce
8 tablespoonsful mayonnaise	½ cupful mayonnaise
1 teaspoonful turmeric	1 teaspoonful turmeric

1. Mix all the ingredients together with a fork.

4.

SOYMILK

Learning how to make soymilk has been a wonderful discovery for me because it is simple and quick to make, and because it is delicious and can be used to make so many things that I had stopped making when I gave up using dairy milk; such things as custards, puddings, ice creams, sauces, etc. These all come out beautifully when made with home-made soymilk. Many people have tasted soymilk which they didn't like, or they may have some unpleasant association with it. The taste is not exactly the same as cow's milk, but when it is freshly made at home with whole soybeans, it is positively delicious, and one can easily adapt to the slightly different taste. I now use it as I would have used cow's milk, quite happily, even on cereals and fruit, not just in cooked dishes in which the flavour of the soymilk is more likely to be masked.

If you have used the recipe for making tofu, you will find this recipe is fun because it takes much less time in comparison; it is, of course, the same process that goes into making soymilk for tofu production (see page 26). The difference is that soymilk for making tofu is thinner than soymilk for using as milk.

Be sure to remember that because this soymilk is thicker than that for tofu making, your sack for pressing the milk out of the okara is a slightly different weave from the one for tofu making. It may take some trial and error to find the best material for the job, but I have found that linen is a good choice. It must be loosely woven enough to allow the thicker milk to go through, but not so loosely woven that the okara goes through as well.

What You Will Need

Strong electric blender/liquidizer which can run steadily for 1½-2 minutes without stopping (some have to be stopped periodically).

Cooking pot (4-5 quarts with lid).

'Pressing pot' or basin with a large round bottomed colander which fits into it.

Source of boiling water — saucepan or electric kettle (you will use about 2 quarts of water, or a little more).

Linen bag which will serve to collect okara and let the soymilk through. I made mine about 23 inches (58cm) wide by about 18 inches (46cm) long with French seams which zig-zag for extra strength because the bag must withstand a fair bit of pressure when you press the hot soymilk through. See the section on making tofu for how to do this.

Long handled spoon for stirring soymilk.

Measuring cup.

Rubber gloves.

Soyabeans — ¾ lb (350g) or 2 cupsful. These must be presoaked about ten hours (see instructions following). Larger beans give a better yield of milk.

Getting Started

Soaking the beans (the night before). Put the beans into a bowl and run cool water over them to fill up the bowl. Pour the water off and refill the bowl while stirring the beans around to release the dirt. Repeat the process until you are sure that the water is clear and the beans are clean — it doesn't take long. Then cover the beans with water, making sure that the water is at least 2 inches (5cm) above the beans because they absorb water and expand during soaking, and you want to find them covered with water in the morning.

A word about water temperature: If the weather is cold, soak the beans in warm water. If you only have 8 hours to soak them, put them into hot water, and if you only have 4 hours put them into boiling water and after a couple of hours pour off the water and refill with boiling water. You will have to work out the timing according to the temperature of your kitchen.

Note: Before grinding the beans must be tested in the same way as in the method for making tofu (see page 26).

Process

1. Divide the beans into three approximately equal portions.

2. Warm blender container by filling with boiling water and leaving to stand for a couple of minutes.

3. Put 1 portion of beans into blender container with 1 pint (½ litre) boiling water. Blend for 2 minutes and pour contents directly into linen bag which is sitting in colander in 'pressing pot'.

4. Repeat procedure with remaining 2 portions of beans.

Note: If you have no blender, you can use a hand grain mill/food mill or even meat grinder if it will grind finely enough. Be sure when using a hand grain mill that it won't be ruined by grinding the moist beans. If all's well you grind the beans as finely as possible in the mill. It may be necessary to grind twice, that is, put the ground beans through the mill a second time to make the grinding come out finer still. Then you pour the ground beans plus an extra 3 pints (1½ litres or 7½ cupsful) of boiling water into the linen bag which is sitting in the colander in the 'pressing pot'.

5. When all the beans have been ground, and the 'go' is poured into the bag, squeeze as much milk through the bag as possible.

6. Open bag and stir okara a little bit, then add 24 fl oz (600ml) or 3 cupsful boiling water to okara and squeeze again to release as much milk as possible. *Be careful not to burn yourself.*

7. When you are satisfied that you have got as much milk from the pulp as you can, pour the milk into the cooking pot, which rests on an asbestos mat or 'flame tamer', and bring the milk to the boil over a medium heat, again watching it carefully and stirring frequently because it boils over easily.

8.   After the milk boils, reduce heat and simmer for 7 minutes, then it is done, ready to use. I like to let it cool and skim off the skin that develops — called yuba — and put it into a bowl and eat it with a pinch of salt and some honey or raisins.

It is a delicious treat. You can increase its shelf-life and improve the flavour if you cool the milk quickly in cold, running water (for instance, by putting the covered pot into the sink and running cold water around the pot — not over top in case the water gets into soymilk — and then putting it into clean bottles and refrigerating it immediately). I do find, however, that when I cool the milk quickly the yuba does not develop in the same way as when the milk cools gradually. Another nice treat is the freshly prepared soymilk taken as a drink with a pinch of salt and a little honey while it is still warm.

Now the soymilk is ready for whatever use you have in mind. I must say that when it comes to making soymilk, I find that it makes all the difference in flavour, colour and consistency to make it directly from the whole beans which you grind yourself. I have made it from soyflour and soymilk powders, and I just don't think that there is any comparison in the taste. I think that it is very quick and simple to make home-made soymilk from the whole beans as I have described. I usually make twice the recipe amount at one time, and then I have it available for many uses, and it keeps for about a week in the refrigerator.

SOYMILK FRENCH TOAST WITHOUT EGGS

Imperial (Metric)
⅓ pint (200ml) soymilk
2 oz (50g) wholewheat flour
½ teaspoonful sea salt
1 tablespoonful honey (optional)
1 tablespoonful arrowroot
4-6 slices of wholewheat bread

American
1 cupful soymilk
½ cupful wholewheat flour
½ teaspoonful sea salt
1 tablespoonful honey (optional)
1 tablespoonful arrowroot
4-6 slices of wholewheat bread

1. Combine all the ingredients except for the bread.

2. Dip the bread in the batter and fry each piece, turning it once until nicely crisped on both sides. Serve with honey, apple sauce, raw sugar, jam or maple syrup.

YEASTY PANCAKES

Imperial (Metric)	American
1 pint (½ litre) soymilk	2½ cupsful soymilk
3 tablespoonsful vegetable oil	4 tablespoonsful vegetable oil
2 tablespoonsful honey	2 tablespoonsful honey
2 tablespoonsful dried yeast or	2 tablespoonsful dried yeast or
3 tablespoonsful fresh yeast	4 tablespoonsful fresh yeast
¾ lb (350g) wholewheat flour	3 cupsful wholewheat flour
1 teaspoonful sea salt	1 teaspoonful sea salt

1. Mix together the liquids and heat them until they are warm — about 100-110°F/37.5-43°C.

2. Add the yeast, flour and salt and set the batter aside for 5-10 minutes.

3. Drop spoonsful of the batter into a greased pan, allow the pancakes to brown on one side, then turn them over and continue cooking until brown on both sides.

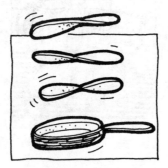

TEMPURA

Tempura is a dish that is so special that it deserves a little in the way of an explanation. Tempura is vegetables or really anything you fancy dipped in batter and deep fried, and it is absolutely delicious. Most people who like tempura enjoy experimenting with various batters, hoping to find the *best* tempura batter, although of course this is a matter of taste and opinion. I have been making tempura for quite a few years now — I learned about it initially in Boston when I was studying macrobiotics. This is one of my favourite tempura batters:

Imperial (Metric)	American
6 oz (150g) wholewheat flour	1½ cupsful wholewheat flour
½-1 teaspoonful sea salt	½-1 teaspoonful sea salt
⅔-¾ pint (330-375ml) cold soymilk	1½-2 cupsful cold soymilk
1½ tablespoonsful arrowroot	1½ tablespoonsful arrowroot

1. Combine the ingredients well, but don't overmix them because otherwise the batter will become more like a dough. (Also make sure that the soymilk is cold — if the ingredients are not cold, it helps to chill the mixture in the fridge for a while before using it.)

2. Cut the vegetables into attractive bite-size pieces, dip them in the batter and deep fry them in the vegetable oil until they are nicely browned. (If you are not serving the tempura immediately, be sure to keep the vegetables warm in an oven which is not hotter than 250°F/130°C (Gas Mark ½). If the oven is on too high a setting the vegetables will go brown and become bitter tasting.)

Note: You can also use tofu for tempura, and it sometimes helps, if the batter doesn't stick too well to the tofu or vegetables, to dip the food in wholewheat flour before putting it into the batter. (This usually isn't necessary, but for particularly smooth or slippery foods it is useful to know.)

WHITE SAUCE

Imperial (Metric)	American
2½ tablespoonsful vegetable oil	3 tablespoonsful vegetable oil
2½ tablespoonsful wholewheat flour	3 tablespoonsful wholewheat flour
½ pint (¼ litre) soymilk	1½ cupsful soymilk
½ teaspoonful sea salt	½ teaspoonful sea salt.

1. Heat the oil in a saucepan, add the flour and cook it for a minute or so.

2. Add the soymilk, stirring it in slowly to avoid lumps of flour forming.

3. Add the salt and simmer the sauce for about 5-10 minutes until the sauce is cooked.

Variations

To make an onion sauce, *sauté* 1 chopped onion in vegetable oil before adding the remaining ingredients.

For a mushroom sauce, *sauté* 1 oz (25g) of sliced mushrooms and follow the recipe as for white sauce.

Add any herbs, curry or chilli powder or cumin for flavouring.

EGGLESS SOYMILK CUSTARD

Imperial (Metric)	American
¾ pint (400ml) soymilk	2 cupsful soymilk
2 tablespoonsful honey	2 tablespoonsful honey
Pinch of sea salt	Pinch of sea salt
1 teaspoonful pure vanilla essence	1 teaspoonful pure vanilla essence
2 tablespoonsful lemon juice, freshly squeezed	2 tablespoonsful lemon juice, freshly squeezed
Nutmeg to taste (optional)	Nutmeg to taste (optional)

1. Heat the soymilk, but don't allow it to boil.

2. Add the honey and salt and stir until they are dissolved.

3. Remove the pan from the heat and stir in the vanilla and lemon juice.

4. Set the pan aside for about half an hour, then place it in the fridge for 1 hour or overnight. Serve this over fruit or cakes and use it as you would a custard sauce.

Note: If you look closely at this recipe, you will see that it makes a flavoured silken tofu, because the lemon juice causes the kind of reaction as it would in tofu making, and the curds are not separated from the whey. This may provide further ideas for using silken tofu.

ICE CREAM BASE

Imperial (Metric)	American
4 oz (100g) honey (or to taste)	½ cupful honey (or to taste)
1¼ pints (650ml) soymilk	3 cupsful soymilk
1-2 teaspoonsful pure vanilla essence or a few drops	1-2 teaspoonsful pure vanilla essence or a few drops
6 tablespoonsful vegetable oil	8 tablespoonsful vegetable oil
¼ teaspoonful sea salt	¼ teaspoonful sea salt

1. Combine the ingredients well and place the mixture in an ice cream maker and freeze it. (Alternatively, leave the mixture in the freezer compartment of the fridge until it begins to set, then beat it again and return it to the freezer to firm up.)

Variations
For carob ice cream, simply add about 4 oz (100g)/1 cupful of carob powder (or according to taste). Carob chips also make a nice variation.

Add any kind of flavour or fruit that you fancy — you can let your imagination take over with this recipe.

RICE PUDDING

Imperial (Metric)	American
1 lb (½ kilo) brown rice, cooked	2 cupsful brown rice, cooked
½ pint (¼ litre) soymilk	1¼ cupsful soymilk
3-5 tablespoonsful honey	4-6 tablespoonsful honey
1 teaspoonful pure vanilla essence or a few drops	1 teaspoonful pure vanilla essence or a few drops
2 eggs (optional)	2 eggs (optional)
2 teaspoonsful lemon juice	2 teaspoonsful lemon juice
1 teaspoonful grated lemon rind	1 teaspoonful grated lemon rind

1. Combine the ingredients, adding a little more soymilk if necessary.

2. Place the pudding mixture into a greased baking dish and bake at 325°F/170°C (Gas Mark 3) for 50 minutes.

EGG CUSTARD SAUCE

Imperial (Metric)	**American**
1 egg, lightly beaten	1 egg, lightly beaten
¼ pint (150ml) soymilk	¾ cupful soymilk
2 tablespoonsful honey	2 tablespoonsful honey
Pinch of sea salt	Pinch of sea salt
1 teaspoonful pure vanilla essence	1 teaspoonful pure vanilla essence

1. Scald the soymilk and leave it to cool slightly.

2. Add the lightly beaten egg, honey and salt, then heat the custard in the top of a double boiler or in a pan on an asbestos mat or flame tamer, stirring all the time until the custard coats the back of a metal spoon.

3. Remove the pan from the heat, add the vanilla and any other flavourings you wish, cool and use it as a dessert sauce.

EGGLESS SWEET CUSTARD

Imperial (Metric)	American
5 tablespoonsful vegetable oil	6 tablespoonsful vegetable oil
5 tablespoonsful wholewheat flour	6 tablespoonsful wholewheat flour
¾ pint (400ml) soymilk	2 cupsful soymilk
1 teaspoonful sea salt	1 teaspoonful sea salt
½ teaspoonful pure vanilla essence	½ teaspoonful pure vanilla essence
3 tablespoonsful honey	4 tablespoonsful honey

1. Heat the oil in a saucepan, add the flour and cook it for about 1 minute.

2. Add the milk slowly while stirring the sauce over a low heat.

3. Add the salt and continue stirring for 5-10 minutes until the sauce thickens and the flour is cooked.

4. Remove the pan from the heat and add the vanilla. Allow the sauce to cool or serve it hot over cakes or fruit desserts.

Variation
Try flavouring the custard with rosemary by infusing a small sprig in the milk while cooking.

SOYMILK CAROB DRINK

Imperial (Metric)	American
Soymilk, hot or cold	Soymilk, hot or cold
Honey to taste	Honey to taste
Carob powder to taste	Carob powder to taste
Pinch of sea salt	Pinch of sea salt

1. Blend all the ingredients in a liquidizer and serve the drink immediately.

5.

OTHER SOYBEAN PRODUCTS

Whey

Whey is the liquid which is separated from the curds after the curdling agent has been added to soymilk in the tofu making process. Whey contains some of the protein plus some of the B vitamins and natural sugar of the dry soybeans. It makes delicious, almost sweet soups when used as the soup stock, and it is a good liquid for making bread because it helps the yeast to rise as a result of the natural sugar in it. I frequently use freshly made whey to moisten and warm animal food. If I have just made tofu, and it is time to feed the cats and dogs in our house, I add some whey to their food, especially if they are having leftovers which have been in the refrigerator long enough to get cold.

Another very interesting way of using whey is in cleaning. It is good for cleaning the tofu making equipment, but I don't usually use it for that because my husband likes to use it in the laundry. In our household, my husband does all the family laundry because he does it so well, and one of the secrets of his success is that he includes a little whey which cleans by cutting through the grease. I turn over all the whey that I can to Philip except for the amount that I put away for use in soups or breadmaking.

Whey can be used as a shampoo because it is a rich source of lecithin which cuts grease quickly. I have used it quite successfully as a shampoo, and we have a friend who has very sensitive skin who finds that she can wash her face with whey, but not with water!

Again, unless one makes tofu at home, whey is not available in this country, although I understand that in some tofu shops in the Far

East the proprietors give the whey to housewives who wish to use it for their daily washing up.

Go

Go is simply a *purée* of soaked soybeans ground with water which is really the first step in tofu or soymilk production. When used as a food in its own right, go has the advantage of being much quicker to cook than soybeans which are left whole. It can be added to casseroles, soups and stews as a thickener; it is used to enrich puddings and breads; it can be made into croquettes or patties; and can even be added to scrambled eggs.

Go is a food which is open to experiment, so it is a good idea to try to develop new and interesting ways of using it. I will give you an example of how I have used it in one of my favourite bread recipes, which I have made with and without go. This is the standard recipe:

Imperial (Metric)	American
2½ tablespoonsful dried yeast or	3 tablespoonsful dried yeast or
6 tablespoonsful fresh yeast	7½ tablespoonsful fresh yeast
5 oz (125g) honey	⅔ cupful honey
Approx. 2 pints (1 litre) warm water	5-6 cupsful warm water
¼ pint (150ml) vegetable oil	⅔ cupful vegetable oil
2 tablespoonsful sea salt (optional)	2 tablespoonsful sea salt (optional)
Juice of 1 lemon	Juice of 1 lemon
3-3½ lb (1½-1¾ kilos) wholewheat flour	12-14 cupsful wholewheat flour
Approx. 6 oz (150g) soyflour	1-2 cupsful soyflour

1. Mix the yeast with the honey and warm water and set it aside for a few minutes to froth up.

2. Add the remaining ingredients and knead the dough with a mixer or by hand for about 10 minutes.

3. This recipe makes about 4 loaves, depending on the size of the tins used. Divide the dough into greased loaf tins until each one is about half full.

4. Set the tins aside in a warm place for 20-30 minutes until the dough rises to the top of the tins.

5. Bake the loaves in a pre-heated oven at 350°F/180°C (Gas Mark 4) for about 35-40 minutes until done.

Note: To make bread with go, first prepare 5 cupsful of go by soaking 1 cupful of soybeans overnight and then blending them with 1 pint (½ litre) of water. Replace the water and soyflour in the recipe above with the go.

I would prefer to use go than shop-bought soyflour because go is always so much fresher than the flour which may have been on the shelf for a fair amount of time. Incidentally, it is said that flour begins to lose its freshness the minute that it is ground and that one should aim not to use flour that is more than two days old — a point worth considering.

I am not going to include other recipes for the use of go in this book, since I feel it is more a matter of adding a little bit to this soup or that stew or the other casserole. I leave it to you to try out go in different ways.

Okara

Okara is a by-product of the tofu or soymilk making process. It is the pulp which is left after the soymilk has been separated off; it is collected in the 'pressing sack' while the milk goes through. Okara is a high-fibre food which retains some of the proportion of the protein of the soybeans. It usually contains about 3.5 per cent protein or roughly half of the protein content of tofu. The amount of protein in okara is roughly the same as the protein content of whole milk and cooked brown rice.

Okara can be made into delicious croquettes or burgers; it can be added to cakes to make them lighter; it can be used roasted as an ingredient in granola (see the recipe on page 96). It mixes well with eggs for scrambled eggs and can be added to pancake batters, bread and biscuit recipes. It also makes a delicious crumble topping for apples (see page 100). One of the most popular ways of using okara is to make a sausage substitute which was first developed by The Farm in Tennessee and is called Soysage (see the recipe on page 95). Okara is also very good as animal fodder because of its protein and fibre content. I frequently add it to leftovers for my dogs and cats who seem to be thriving on it.

In the Far East, okara has been used for many things from enriching the milk of nursing mothers, to curing diarrhoea, to waxing and polishing household woodwork when it is wrapped in a cloth and rubbed over wooden furniture.

I also enjoy using okara in cake recipes which can be made without eggs because of the light quality of the okara. If you buy tofu commercially and don't make it yourself, you don't get the opportunity to use okara; some people prefer okara to tofu, so that they might wish to make soymilk just to get the okara.

OKARA SOYSAGE

Imperial (Metric)	American
1½ lb (¾ kilo) okara	3 cupsful okara
1 onion, finely chopped	1 onion, finely chopped
1 stick of celery, finely chopped	1 stick of celery, finely chopped
1 apple, finely chopped	1 apple, finely chopped
1 tablespoonful mixed herbs	1 tablespoonful mixed herbs
½ lb (¼ kilo) wholewheat flour	2 cupsful wholewheat flour
3 tablespoonsful natural soy sauce	3 tablespoonsful natural soy sauce
A few tablespoonsful soymilk or water as necessary	A few tablespoonsful soymilk or water as necessary

1. Combine all the ingredients well, adding just enough liquid to make a dough that holds together well.

2. Pack the mixture into a greased bowl or pudding basin with a lid for steaming.

3. Pressure cook the mixture in about 1½ inches of water for 45 minutes, steam it for a couple of hours, or pack it into a loaf tin set in a large baking tin of water and bake it at 350°F/180°C (Gas Mark 4) for about 30-45 minutes.

Note: This delicious recipe may be varied in many ways. The vegetables and fruit may be omitted or replaced by other herbs and spices such as oregano, garlic, cumin, basil, cayenne, wet mustard, black pepper, or allspice.

USING ROASTED OKARA

Place some okara in a dry tin (that is without oil) and roast it for about 1 hour at 300°F/150°C (Gas Mark 4). This may be used in breads and cakes to replace no more than about one quarter of the flour to give a lighter texture. It can also be used this way in croquettes, biscuits, etc.

As a topping for desserts or an ingredient in granola, prepare the okara as follows:

Imperial (Metric)	American
8 tablespoonsful vegetable oil	½ cupful vegetable oil
½ lb (¼ kilo) honey	1 cupful honey
¼ teaspoonful sea salt	¼ teaspoonful sea salt
1 tablespoonful pure vanilla essence	1 tablespoonful pure vanilla essence
2 lb (1 kilo) okara	4 cupsful okara

1. Heat the oil and honey together until they are well mixed.

2. Add the salt and vanilla, pour the mixture over the okara, then put it all into a greased tin and bake it for 1 hour at 300°F/150°C (Gas Mark 2).

OKARA BURGERS

Imperial (Metric)	American
½ lb (¼ kilo) okara	1 cupful okara
1 egg or	1 egg or
4 tablespoonsful soymilk	¼ cupful soymilk
4 oz (100g) wholewheat flour	1 cupful wholewheat flour
1 small onion, minced	1 small onion, minced
1 stick of celery, finely chopped	1 stick of celery, finely chopped
1 tablespoonful natural soy sauce	1 tablespoonful natural soy sauce
½ teaspoonful mixed herbs	½ teaspoonful mixed herbs

1. Combine all the ingredients and knead them well.

2. Form the mixture into patties and deep fry or shallow fry them as convenient.

Note: Use this recipe only as a guideline; substitute or add other vegetables such as grated carrot, spring onions or garlic and use other flavourings such as curry powder, cummin or chilli powder.

ORANGE OKARA CAKE

Imperial (Metric)	American
½ lb (¼ kilo) wholewheat flour	2 cupsful wholewheat flour
1 tablespoonful baking powder	1 tablespoonsful baking powder
1 teaspoonful sea salt	1 teaspoonful sea salt
1 tablespoonful grated orange rind	1 tablespoonful grated orange rind
4 oz (100g) chopped almonds	1 cupful chopped almonds
5 oz (125g) sultanas	1 cupful sultanas
1 lb (½ kilo) okara	2 cupsful okara
4 tablespoonsful vegetable oil	¼ cupful vegetable oil
¾ pint (400ml) soymilk	2 cupsful soymilk
1 lb (½ kilo) honey	1¼ cupsful honey
2 teaspoonsful pure almond essence	2 teaspoonsful pure almond essence

1. Combine the ingredients thoroughly, adding the wet ingredients to the dry ingredients and then adding the nuts and sultanas.

2. Turn the mixture into a greased cake tin or fairy cake tins.

3. Bake at 350°F/180°C (Gas Mark 4) for about 30 minutes. If desired, make a mixture of 4 oz (100g or ½ cupful) of butter or vegetable margarine, 4 oz (100g or ⅓ cupful) of honey and 8 tablespoonsful of pure orange juice to spread on the cake after it has been removed from the oven.

BANANA OKARA BREAD

Imperial (Metric)	American
½ oz (15g) fresh yeast or	½ tablespoonful fresh yeast or
2 teaspoonsful dried yeast	2 teaspoonsful dried yeast
½ lb (¼ kilo) honey	1 cupful honey
4 tablespoonsful warm soymilk	¼ cupful warm soymilk
3 bananas, mashed	3 bananas, mashed
4 oz (100g) okara	½ cupful okara
8 tablespoonsful vegetable oil	½ cupful vegetable oil
½ teaspoonful sea salt	½ teaspoonful sea salt
1 egg (optional)	1 egg (optional)
10 oz (300g) wholewheat flour	2½ cupsful wholewheat flour
2 tablespoonsful wheatgerm	¼ cupful wheatgerm
5 oz (125g) raisins	1 cupful raisins
4 oz (100g) chopped nuts	1 cupful chopped nuts

1. Combine the yeast with the honey and soymilk and set the mixture for a few minutes for the yeast to froth up.

2 Add the mashed bananas, okara, oil, salt and egg (if used), and mix them well.

3. Add the flour, wheatgerm, raisins and nuts, combine them well and put the dough into a greased bread tin. Bake the bread at 350°F/180°C (Gas Mark 4) for about 45 minutes.

APPLE CRUMBLE

Imperial (Metric)	American
6-7 apples	6-7 apples
6 tablespoonsful honey	8 tablespoonsful honey
4 oz (100g) vegetable oil or butter	½ cupful vegetable oil or butter
6 oz (150g) wholewheat flour	1½ cupsful wholewheat flour
Pinch of sea salt	Pinch of sea salt
4 teaspoonsful cinnamon	4 teaspoonsful cinnamon
6 oz (150g) okara	¾ cupful okara

1. Slice the apples and place them in a greased baking dish, and trickle the honey over them.

2. Combine the butter or oil, flour, salt, remaining honey, cinnamon and okara and sprinkle the mixture over the apples.

3. Bake the crumble at 375°F/190°C (Gas Mark 5) for 30 minutes.

Note: If the apples are sweet, do not mix any honey with them but use a little in the crumble.

OKARA CAROB CAKE

Imperial (Metric)
4 oz (100g) wholewheat flour
4 oz (100g) carob flour
¾ pint (400ml) soymilk
¾ lb (350g) honey
1 tablespoonful baking powder
1 teaspoonful sea salt
4 tablespoonsful vegetable oil
1 teaspoonful pure vanilla essence

American
1 cupful wholwheat flour
1 cupful carob flour
2 cupsful soymilk
1½ cupsful honey
1 tablespoonful baking powder
1 teaspoonful sea salt
¼ cupful vegetable oil
1 teaspoonful pure vanilla essence

1. Combine the ingredients well.

2. Turn the mixture into a greased cake tin and bake it in the oven for about 45 minutes at 350°F/180°C (Gas Mark 4).

OKARA YEAST COFFEE CAKE

Imperial (Metric)	American
1 oz (25g) fresh yeast or	1 tablespoonful fresh yeast or
½ oz (15g) dried yeast	½ tablespoonful dried yeast
4 oz (100g) honey	½ cupful honey
Approx. ½ pint (¼ litre) warm soymilk	1¼ cupsful warm soymilk
Juice of 1 lemon	Juice of 1 lemon
1 teaspoonful grated lemon rind	1 teaspoonful grated lemon rind
½ lb (¼ kilo) butter or vegetable oil or half and half	1 cupful butter or vegetable oil or half and half
2 teaspoonsful sea salt	2 teaspoonsful sea salt
1¼-1½ lb (575g-¾ kilo) wholewheat flour flour	5-6 cupsful wholewheat
½ lb (¼ kilo) okara	1 cupful okara

1. Combine the yeast, honey and warm milk and set the mixture aside for a few minutes for the yeast to froth up.

2. Add the lemon juice, lemon rind, butter or oil, salt, flour and okara.

3. Beat the mixture well in a cake mixer or by hand for 5-10 minutes.

Filling No. 1

Imperial (Metric)	American
6 oz (150g) ground almonds	1 cupful ground almonds
4 oz (100g) okara	½ cupful okara
1½ oz (40g) wholewheat breadcrumbs	½ cupful wholewheat breadcrumbs
½ teaspoonful cinnamon	½ teaspoonful cinnamon
2 oz (50g) honey	¼ cupful honey
4 tablespoonsful melted butter or vegetable oil	¼ cupful melted butter or vegetable oil
½ teaspoonful sea salt	½ teaspoonful sea salt

Filling No. 2

Imperial (Metric)	American
4 oz (100g) honey	½ cupful honey
4 oz (100g) chopped walnuts	1 cupful chopped walnuts
5 oz (125g) raisins	1 cupful raisins
½ teaspoonful cinnamon	½ teaspoonful cinnamon
½ teaspoonful mixed spice	½ teaspoonful mixed spice

1. Divide the cake mixture into two and turn half into a greased cake tin, spreading either of the fillings on top of the first layer. (For Filling No. 2 sprinkle the ingredients over in the order given and vary the quantities according to taste.)

2. Cover the filling with another layer of the cake mixture and bake it at 350°F/180°C (Gas Mark 4) for about half an hour.

FRUIT BREAD

Imperial (Metric)	American
2 oz (50g) fresh yeast or	2 tablespoonsful fresh yeast or
1 oz (25g) dried yeast	1 tablespoonful dried yeast
4 oz (100g) honey	½ cupful honey
1¼ pints (650ml) warm water or whey	3 cupsful warm water or whey
8 tablespoonsful vegetable oil	½ cupful vegetable oil
2 teaspoonsful sea salt	2 teaspoonsful sea salt
½ lb (¼ kilo) okara	1 cupful okara
1 egg or	1 egg or
4 oz (100g) tofu, blended	½ cupful tofu, blended
2-2¼ lb (1 kilo) wholewheat flour	8-9 cupsful wholewheat flour
1 lb (½ kilo) sultanas	3 cupsful sultanas
4 oz (100g) raisins	¾ cupful raisins
4 oz (100g) currants	¾ cupful currants

1. Mix the yeast with the honey and half the warm water and set it aside for a few minutes for the yeast to froth up.

2. Add the oil, salt, okara and egg and the rest of the warm water (or the tofu blended with the water).

3. Add the flour and dried fruit and mix the ingredients well by hand or with a cake mixer (using the dough hook).

4. Half fill 3 or 4 bread tins and let the dough rise until it reaches the top of the tins.

5. Bake the loaves for about 40 minutes at 350°F/180°C (Gas Mark 4).

Yuba

Yuba is the skin which develops on the soymilk while it is warm, very like the skin on dairy milk with which people are generally more familiar. In the Far East, it is considered a special food which is sold in shops either freshly made or dried. It is a very nutritious food which contains over 50 per cent protein, has a high mineral content and is rich in natural oils and natural sugars. In its dried form, it is a popular high-energy food for campers. In any form, it is recommended to pregnant women and nursing mothers because it is such a highly nutritious food.

I usually enjoy the yuba that develops when I make home-made soymilk. It is my favourite treat during the process of making soymilk. I let the soymilk cool, and when the skin forms, I lift it off carefully with a spoon and put it into a bowl, then I eat it there and then while it is still fresh and warm with a pinch of sea salt and some raisins or honey.

If you want to make yuba yourself, you can use freshly made soymilk and put it into a saucepan on an asbestos mat or into a double boiler. You will need to keep the milk warm, but not boiling — about 175°F/79°C on a cooking thermometer. When a good layer of yuba forms on top of the milk, free it from the pan by cutting around the edges, and then slip a slotted spoon or chopstick under the middle of it, and lift it out carefully. (You can let the yuba cool as it hangs over the spoon or chopstick.)

It takes about 7-8 minutes for a skin to form, so if you keep the soymilk warm in this way, you will get several sheets of yuba. Put about 1½-2 inches of soymilk into the pan for this purpose, and if you want to get a greater yield of yuba, start out with rich soymilk. You make that by reducing the water proportion in the original soymilk recipe. You could use just ¾ pint (400ml) of water in each of the three grindings, and you could then add ¼ pint (150ml) water after you have extracted the first milk from the okara when you would normally add 1¼ pints of boiling water. Rich soymilk is also good for making silken tofu and soymilk yogurt — follow the recipe for ordinary yogurt, but substitute rich soymilk and see how it turns out.

Soynuts

I am including a recipe for making soynuts because they are very tasty and because it sometimes happens that one has soaked soybeans with the intention of making tofu or soymilk, only to find that there isn't enough time to do so, and were it not for soynuts, the beans might be wasted unless you just wanted to cook them as beans. You can experiment in many different ways with flavourings to make the soynuts more interesting.

1. Soak the soybeans overnight as you would if making tofu or soymilk.

2. If you are deep frying the beans, drain them and dry them thoroughly between layers of absorbent towels for about 1 hour.

3. Drop the soybeans about ½ cupful at a time into the hot oil (375°F/190°C) and cook them until they are browned — about 8-10 minutes.

4. Remove the beans from the oil and drain them on absorbent towels.

5. Sprinkle the beans with sea salt and any herbs or flavourings you wish (e.g. garlic, dill weed, mixed herbs and onion powder).

Note: The soybeans may also be roasted: after draining the soaking water off them, place them in a well greased baking tin and put them in the oven at 250°F/130°C (Gas Mark ½) for about 45 minutes. Check them from time to time, shaking the tin to prevent the beans burning. Take the beans out of the oven when they are soft. Don't let them become dark brown because they turn bitter then.

6.
SOYBEANS AS BEANS

Many people do not know how to use soybeans just as beans, and they can be most delicious eaten this way if they are cooked properly, so for those of you who wish to use them as they are, I have included this chapter. Another reason for giving you a few recipes using soybeans as beans is that I realize there are many people who may be intrigued by the idea of making tofu and soymilk but who would be more likely to make use of whole soybeans in their cooking.

For each cupful of soaked soybeans use 2½ cupsful or 1 pint (¼ litre) of water and pressure cook the beans for about 25 minutes. Be sure to drain off the soaking water, and use 1 pint of fresh water for cooking. It is helpful to add 2 tablespoonsful of vegetable oil or margarine to prevent the beans clogging the vent pipe of the pressure cooker. If you don't have a pressure cooker, you can cook them in a saucepan, but you should then use about 3 pints (1½ litres) of water, and make sure that the water in the saucepan is kept up. You could put in 2 pints (1 litre) of water when you start cooking, then cook the beans for several hours and add more water when necessary, checking every half hour or so until the beans are done. When they are done, they can be easily crushed between your tongue and the roof of your mouth or between the thumb and ring finger. Soybeans can be pressure cooked without soaking, but I prefer them after they have been soaked. If you want to pressure cook them without soaking, you need to use 1 pint (½ litre) of water per ½ lb (¼ kilo) of soybeans and cook them for about 1½ hours.

Once the beans are cooked, you can add a variety of flavourings, or leave them as they are and use them in soups, stews, burgers or whatever. Here are some suggestions of possible flavourings that you might enjoy: miso, natural soy sauce, sea salt, lemon juice, butter, honey, molasses, garlic or onion (minced), vegetables on their own or in combination, curry powder, dill weed, mixed herbs, tahini, peanut butter or cheese.

If you have pre-cooked soybeans available, you can easily add them to various dishes in your daily cooking.

SOYBURGERS

Imperial (Metric)	American
1 lb (½ kilo) soybeans, cooked, drained and mashed	2 cupsful soybeans, cooked, drained and mashed
½ lb (¼ kilo) brown rice	1 cupful brown rice
1 onion, minced	1 onion, minced
1 small carrot, grated	1 small carrot, grated
4 oz (100g) wholewheat breadcrumbs	2 cupsful wholewheat breadcrumbs
2 tablespoonsful natural soy sauce	2 tablespoonsful natural soy sauce
1 egg or	1 egg or
¼ pint (150ml) soymilk	¾ cupful soymilk
2 oz (50g) wholewheat flour	½ cupful wholewheat flour
Seasoning to taste (e.g. herbs, garlic or curry powder, cumin)	Seasoning to taste (e.g. herbs, garlic or curry powder, cumin)
Vegetable oil for frying	Vegetable oil for frying

1. Combine all the ingredients together and knead the mixture for a couple of minutes to bind it.

2. Form the mixture into patties and deep fry or shallow fry them in the oil, turning them once.

CURRIED BEANBALLS WITH
SWEET AND SOUR SAUCE

Imperial (Metric)	American
½ lb (¼ kilo) soybeans, pre-cooked	1 cupful soybeans, pre-cooked
⅓ pint (200ml) water or bean cooking liquid	1 cupful water or bean cooking liquid
1 onion, minced	1 onion, minced
6 oz (150g) wholewheat flour	1½ cupsful wholewheat flour
1 teaspoonful sea salt	1 teaspoonful sea salt
1½ teaspoonsful curry powder	1½ teaspoonsful curry powder
1 tablespoonful baking powder	1 tablespoonful baking powder
Vegetable oil for frying	Vegetable oil for frying

1. Mash the soybeans and add the remaining ingredients, mixing them thoroughly.

2. Drop spoonsful of the mixture into the hot oil for deep frying and cook them for 2-3 minutes. (The oil should be kept at about 350°F/180°C).

Sweet and Sour Sauce

Imperial (Metric)	American
2 onions, chopped	2 onions, chopped
Vegetable oil for frying	Vegetable oil for frying
2 tablespoonsful natural soy sauce	2 tablespoonsful natural soy sauce
1 green pepper, chopped	1 green pepper, chopped
2 tomatoes, chopped	2 tomatoes, chopped
1 small tin tomato paste	1 small tim tomato paste
2 medium-sized tins pineapple in its own juice	2 medium-sized tins pineapple in its own juice
2 tablespoonsful honey	2 tablespoonsful honey
2½ tablespoonsful cider vinegar	3 tablespoonsful cider vinegar
⅓ pint (200ml) water	1 cupful water
1 tablespoonful arrowroot	1 tablespoonful arrowroot

1. *Sauté* the onions in the oil in a large pan for a few minutes until the onions are softened.

2. Add the remaining ingredients, except for the water and arrowroot, and cook the sauce for a few more minutes until the vegetables are well mixed.

3. Dissolve the arrowroot thoroughly in the water, add it to the mixture and let it cook for another couple of minutes until the white arrowroot liquid thickens and becomes clear. Serve the sauce hot.

7.

FOOD VALUE OF SOYFOODS

If one were to set about inventing a food which contained all the elements that we in the West prize as important in our diet, and which didn't contain the ones which we have decided were detrimental, one would be hard pressed to come up with something to fit that requirement better than tofu and soymilk and the other foods which are made from them.

Tofu is rich in high-quality protein which is equal to that of milk and eggs when used on its own, and when it is combined with grains or bread, the amount of protein which is able to be used by the body is increased substantially as a result of the combination. (See *Diet for a Small Planet* by Frances Moore Lappe, published by Ballantine Books.) If we were to look at tables of percentages of protein in various foods, we would find that tofu ranks slightly above brown rice and whole milk, and that it has just over half the percentage of protein found in hamburger, eggs and wholewheat flour. It has more than one-third the percentage of protein found in beef, chicken, fish and cottage cheese. Interestingly, highest on the list of protein percentage are not the animal foods as mentioned, but instead, they are such things as soybeans, soyflour, yuba and dried-frozen tofu.

More important than the percentage of protein that exists in a food is the percentage of protein that the body is actually able to use, and this measurement is expressed in a percentage called the 'Net Protein Utilization' or NPU. It is the NPU that is more meaningful to us as 'eaters'. A food may have a high percentage of protein, but if it also has inhibiting factors which make the food difficult to digest and which prevent our bodies from making full use of the protein it does contain, then we are not getting the full benefit of that protein.

As an aside, it has happened that a good deal of the testing of food value of soyfoods has been done on rats, and from the results of those tests scientists have estimated what the results would have been in the case of human consumption of soyfoods. By this method, certain inaccuracies were discovered which showed that soyfoods were actually of more value to humans than had previously been thought. I suppose that it is more convenient to test foods on rats, whose needs may be similar in some ways to ours, although they are obviously not exactly the same; very few people would be interested in spending their days in laboratory cages testing foods even in the interest of science!

When the comparative figures of NPU are examined, we find that tofu rates slightly higher on the scale than chicken, soybeans and soyflour and slightly lower than oatmeal, beef and hamburger. Highest on this list are brown rice, cottage cheese, fish and eggs. In terms of the actual percentage of protein tofu has only about one-third of the protein of chicken and beef, and we find the NPU of tofu is actually higher than that of chicken but only slightly lower than that of beef and hamburger (taken from *Diet for a Small Planet* and *The Book of Tofu*). It works out that a ½ lb (¼ kilo) serving of tofu can give the same amount of usable protein as about 3 oz (75g) of steak or 5 oz (125g) of minced beef, and when one considers that, at the time of writing, one pays about 29p (Irish) per pound of soybeans (which yield about 2 lbs 1 kilo of tofu), I think that it is clear that tofu is a far cheaper source of protein than meat, and that the quality of the protein is comparable. Not only is tofu a much less expensive source of protein than meat, but it has fewer calories and no cholesterol.

Another aspect of protein foods that should be considered is that many people find that one or several of the usual protein foods such as meats, dairy products, eggs and even beans are difficult, if not impossible, to digest; an adequate substitute for those foods is therefore in great demand. Tofu is 95 per cent digestible because the process to make it removes the crude fibre and water-soluble carbohydrates from the soybeans. It is therefore a super food for babies, elderly people, people with specific digestive difficulties, invalids, convalescents, indeed everyone.

Up to now, I have been considering the protein value of tofu as a food on its own, but it is rare that one eats a food on its own, and thanks to the work of Frances Moore Lappe in her book, *Diet for a Small Planet*, we now know that by combining foods wisely, we can substantially increase the amount of protein which is available to the body. In the case of tofu, if we eat it with grains, bread, peanut butter or tahini, we can further increase the amount of available protein from between 10-30 per cent. In the years that I have been using tofu, I cannot think of many occasions, if any, when I have eaten tofu without some form of grain or bread, so that by using tofu in a perfectly acceptable, tasty and normal way, the meal's protein content is further increased without the need for any kind of animal protein.

The reason for the substantial increase in protein available to the body is the fact that while tofu contains the right essential amino acids (indeed soybeans are the only beans with the full complement of these acids), it has proportionately less of the sulphur-containing amino acids, methionine and cystine which are well supplied in grains. Grains, on the other hand, have a rather small amount of lysine which is generously supplied in tofu, so that when the two are put together, they complement each other and the result is an increase in the available protein. The protein in the body is made up of 22 amino acids, eight of which cannot be synthesized by the body and must be therefore be obtained from outside sources. In order for the body to absorb and digest these eight essential amino acids, they must be present at the same time and in the right proportions. So, while tofu has a high protein content on its own, the addition of grains simply serves to make the best use of the protein in both foods.

Tofu is a good source of minerals. It has more calcium than cow's milk which makes its a very valuable food in countries where other high-calcium foods are not eaten regularly, either because they are not available or because people cannot afford them. It is also a good source of iron, but there is now some question as to whether or not the iron is able to be absorbed by the body. It contains potassium, B vitamins, choline, vitamin E and phosphorous. Furthermore, tofu is very low in sodium compared to meat and dairy foods and this is another important consideration when salt or sodium is rapidly gaining a bad reputation as far as diet is concerned.

Many people are very concerned about the acid/alkaline balance of food, that is its pH factor. While most protein foods have an acid reaction in the body, tofu has a almost alkaline reaction with a pH of about 6.5.

Those people who are afraid of using beans or bean products because of flatulence will be pleased to learn that the process of making both tofu and tempeh removes any of the components which contribute to the production of wind or flatus.

Another important point is that not only is tofu made in the traditional way without the use of preservatives, but during the growing stage, soybeans retain less in the way of agricultural chemicals than do animals which are used as food. When comparing meat, fish, poultry and dairy foods to legumes with regard to pesticide residues which are found in them, we find that legumes have the least, dairy products have more and meat, fish and poultry have the most. It seems that these chemical residues concentrate in the fatty tissues of the animals.

There is a real concern about cholesterol, fat and calories in food today. Once again, tofu comes out a winner. Tofu is low in saturated fat, and it has no cholesterol at all. Anybody who must be on a low-fat, low-cholesterol diet will find tofu a very valuable food indeed. Last but certainly not least is the fact that tofu is so low in calories relative to other high-protein foods. It has less than half the number of calories of eggs and about one-quarter the number of calories of an equal portion of beef.

I think that I should, once again, mention the cost of tofu, soymilk and indeed any soybean foods. During the current recession when incomes are not keeping pace with inflation, it is becoming more and more difficult to ensure a high-quality diet based on the traditional foods; meat, poultry, dairy foods and fish are all becoming more expensive at a faster rate than are grains, beans, and vegetables. Therefore, it is extremely good news to hear of an inexpensive food which can supply high-quality protein without the disadvantages of fat, cholesterol and chemical residues.

Soymilk is an important soybean food. It has more iron than cow's milk; fewer calories (about half); no sodium; about one-sixth the amount of calcium; about equal protein; less fat (about half) and far fewer chemical residues. It has rather similar amounts of B vitamins and no cholesterol, and it is very easy to digest. It also has an alkaline reaction in the body.

Soymilk has been used extensively in infant feeding, and it is especially valuable to infants for whom there is no possibility of being breast-fed or who suffer from lactose intolerance. Lactose intolerance, or allergy to cow's milk, seems to be increasing in our society. Few people would deny that mother's milk is the best choice for infant feeding, but failing that, there are the possibilities of soymilk and/or grain milk which can provide perfectly adequate nourishment for infants.

In my research into the use of soymilk for infant feeding, I was very much hoping that I could find information which would enable me to say that if you added certain foods or vitamins to your home-made soymilk it would be suitable for infant feeding. I have come across some varied opinions and recommendations, including suggestions to add such things as malt, very finely ground oatmeal, calcium, vitamin B2 or honey. One nutritionist claims that soymilk can be used on its own, but must be diluted if the infant is very young because of its very high protein content. It is a fact that many infants have been raised successfully on soymilk formulas, but I can make no recommendations because I am not a doctor and have no experience in this area.

I must mention, however, that there are commercially prepared infant formulas. In the early days of creating formulas from soy, they were made from soy flour, but now there are several brands made from soy protein isolates which are prepared from the high-protein, defatted soymeal produced when the soy oil has been removed from the crushed soybeans. These formulas are very reliable, medically approved and tested and can be used if necessitated by the absence of mother's milk.

Okara has less than half the protein of tofu and also less than half the fat. It has slightly less iron than a hamburger; it has no sodium, about twice the amount of potassium in tofu, and it has some of the B vitamins. Its most important contribution to the diet is in its fibre. It has even fewer calories than tofu.

Whey receives about nine per cent of the protein of the original soybeans, some of the natural sugars and a supply of B vitamins; it has a good supply of lecithin which is why it easily cuts grease for cleaning and washing up.

Yuba is a very concentrated food which is high in protein, minerals and fat. It is a delicious speciality food.

When one looks at the food value of soyfoods, it is easy to see how they have been invaluable as a most important source of high-quality protein for many years in areas of high population concentration such as China and Japan.

8.

THE HISTORY OF THE SOYBEAN

The earliest records of the use of soybeans as food come from China as far back as 1100 B.C. The Japanese have used soybeans for nearly as long, starting about 500 B.C. In such countries with a problem of overpopulation, the highly respected soybean was almost the only source of high-quality protein for the people. No wonder it was regarded as one of the five 'sacred grains' (rice, wheat, millet and barley being the others). Of these five, it was the soybean which yielded the largest amount of protein. How wise these people were to rely on the soybean which can produce over 30 per cent protein per acre of land than any other known crop. About 18 times as much usable protein can be produced on an acre of land devoted to growing soybeans than on one used for grazing beef cattle or growing their food!

Soybeans were introduced to Europe and America in the late 1700s or early 1800s, but it took about 110 more years before there was much interest generated in them. Even when interest grew, people took them to be more suitable for animal feeding than for human food. In Europe, more especially England or the British Isles, it has been felt that the climate is just not warm enough to grow soybeans. There have been strains of soybeans developed which have grown successfully in Canada, Sweden and Russia, so perhaps there will eventually be one which will grow well in the British Isles. Then it will just be a matter of finding enough available land for the growing of them.

In America, results have been dramatically different. From a very small beginning in the latter half of the 1890s, production has grown to such heights that America is now the largest producer of soybeans in the world; in fact, more soybeans are now produced in America than in all the other countries of the world combined. The rapid growth of the soybean industry in America came as a result of a number of factors, not the least of which was the climate, which was ideal for the production of soybeans in the large farming areas of America. However, it needed more than a good climate for soybean production to grow from nothing at the turn of the century to over 60 per cent of the world crop now.

One of the most distinguished and persistent pioneers in creating this soybean industry was William Joseph Morse who was born in the latter half of the nineteenth century and who died in 1959. He dedicated his life to encouraging the industry and educating the American people about growing and using soybeans. He worked for the US Department of Agriculture, and spent time developing and testing various types of soybeans and then passing them on to farmers for further testing. He wrote numerous articles and a classic book, co-authored by Dr Charles Piper, called *The Soybean*. He helped to found the American Soybean Association and to carry on more research and development within the association. He spent a couple of years in East Asia further researching soybeans and their use in foods, collecting samples of several thousand varieties of soybeans, learning more about the growing methods and technology of soybean production, and collecting samples of foods made from soybeans. His time in East Asia further inspired him regarding the potentials of the soybean, so that when he returned to the USA, he redoubled his efforts toward establishing the American interest in soybeans. He expanded his work with the USDA and encouraged researchers at the University of Illinois to carry on research with soyfoods which has continued since that time. Because of his strong dedication and singleness of purpose, he is thought to be one of the men responsible for establishing the American soybean industry.

Another pioneer of soybeans in the West was Dr Harry Miller who spent a good deal of time not only developing soymilk and other soyfoods in America, but pioneering the use of soymilk in China, especially for infant feeding. Before this time, the Chinese had been eating tofu regularly, but they had not really begun to drink soymilk as a beverage. Dr Miller and his son established the first soy dairy in the world in Shanghai in 1936. The soymilk in various flavours became so popular that soon there developed a delivery route throughout the city of Shanghai. Unfortunately, the plant was destroyed by bombs just eight months after it opened. Dr Miller then returned to America and set up a soy dairy in Mt Vernon, Ohio. Because soymilk did not become popular in America nearly so quickly as it had in China, he developed other soybean foods and worked with Ohio State University on research and development of different kinds of foods made from soybeans. Interestingly, at that time, in the early 1940s, Kellogg Battle Greek Food Company was also involved in manufacturing soyfoods.

Using soymilk for infant feeding in China had been very successful around the time of 1926 because there were so many orphans there and not enough wet nurses to feed them all. Dairy milk was very expensive and in short supply, so soymilk became their life line; the interest from the general public grew from that. The situation in America in the 1940s, however, was quite different because babies were being fed cows' milk very successfully, and people were not interested in trying the soy-based product, despite the fact that Miller felt that soymilk was better for babies than cows' milk. He was disappointed that the American people did not eagerly accept his soymilk product since he felt that by using soymilk people would be making more efficient use of the land, thereby enabling more people to be fed. He also knew that soymilk was cheaper and more healthful than cows' milk. Nevertheless, soymilk did become more popular in time, although it is still not a regular item on the average American's shopping list, and this fact must have a great deal to do with the fact that it is not readily available; there are rarely any bottles or cartons of soymilk in the refrigerated cases of most supermarkets. In all fairness, it may be that one of the reasons that soymilk did not rise in popularity quickly was because it was usually sold in powdered form which is not nearly so delicious as it is when sold as milk made from whole soybeans with perhaps some honey or malt to flavour it.

Dr Miller concentrated on the use of soybeans as food and not on the agricultural side of the project as did Morse. He continued a medical practice and helped people throughout the world to establish soy dairies. He also directed hospitals and sanitariums in the Far East on several ocasions, and he worked with the people at Loma Linda University, a Seventh Day Adventist University in Southern California which has done much to promote soyfoods as well because the Seventh Day Adventists aim for dietary reform and tend to be vegetarian as part of their belief.

With the help of those two men, Dr Harry Miller and William Morse among others, the tremendous soybean industry in America grew and developed. There is one more man who deserves a mention in this context, and it is Henry Ford who spent money on the research into and development of soy protein for industrial use, especially with regard to plastics, although he also concerned himself with food uses. He encouraged the growing of soybeans in Michigan, and he showed an understanding and appreciation of the potential of the soybean. Even with the work that these dedicated people put into the project, a large percentage of soybeans is still used for making soyoil and for feeding livestock. A large proportion of the population in the West has not yet recognized the value of soybeans when used as human food. The same is true of grains which are far more frequently fed to animals than to people. If the grains and beans which are grown in America were used directly as human food, a large amount of the protein which is irretrievably lost to the animal's metabolism and is not passed on to those who actually eat the animal, could be made available to more people.

But do not despair — help is on the way. There is a whole new wave of people and organizations which are working towards educating the public in the use of soyfoods, and that is most encouraging. In the early 1970s, a vegetarian religious community called The Farm established itself on farmland in Tennessee and the people involved have done a lot of experimenting on soybean foods because they use no animal foods at all. They have published a wonderful cookbook called *The Farm Vegetarian Cookbook* as well as other booklets and leaflets which are helpful for people learning to use soybeans as human food.

In 1975, *The Book of Tofu* by William Shurtleff and Akiko Aoyagi (Mr and Mrs Bill Shurtleff) was published; this is a beautiful, most enlightening and comprehensive look at tofu as a food. It is published by Autumn Press and contains 500 recipes; in 1979, a smaller pocket edition, revised and updated and containing 250 recipes, was published by Ballantine Books. At the time of publication, the authors listed their address in Lafayette, California in the books, so that people could contact them with further questions. They have now created The Soyfood Centre at that address for the purpose of disseminating more information. In 1976 they published *The Book of Miso* with 400 recipes, and in 1979 they published *The Book of Tempeh* with 130 recipes. Also in 1979 they published a most comprehensive volume called *Tofu and Soymilk Production* which is an instruction manual for setting up a factory, soyfood shop or delicatessen.

The publication of these books was most important in changing the direction of the use of soybeans. Now there are several more cookbooks available as well as *Soyfoods*, a quarterly technical trade journal published by the Soy Association of North America which provides information for manufacturers of soy products and other interested people. SANA (The Soy Association of North America) was founded in 1978. It serves as an information centre and trade organization and is ably run by Richard Leviton who works diligently to keep the information available and up to date, and who also organizes annual conferences on soyfoods at which people can both learn more about them and be served them in the delicious meals that are provided.

As a result of the information which is now available, many Americans have started their own soyfood business. Prior to 1970, there were soyfood businesses which were run mostly by Orientals living in America and which were catering largely for the Oriental population in the traditional way. Quong Hop in San Francisco, is one of the oldest and largest tofu/soymilk shops in America. It was started in 1915, and today it produces a variety of soyfoods. Hinode in Los Angeles is the largest soybean shop in America now, and it began in the 1930s in Hawaii and moved to LA later. There were others throughout the USA but not many. One of the largest non-Oriental tofu manufacturers in the USA is the New England Soy Dairy which began in 1976 and which is expanding rapidly. Richard Leviton, director of SANA, was one of the founders of the New England Soy Dairy which began as a corner tofu shop called The Laughing Grasshopper. In 1977, more non-Oriental tofu plants were born; there was White Wave of Boulder, Colorado; Island Spring of Vashon, Washington; Northern Soy in Rochester, New York; The Soy Plant in Ann Arbor, Michigan to name just a few. In 1979, the Tempeh Works started in Massachusetts, and the Ohio Miso Company, which recently moved to Massachusetts, also began. There are many more and some companies in the natural food business are already making a number of soy-based foods for commercial distribution. Health Valley is one, and a company called The Garden of Eatin in California produces a number of delicious soy-based foods.

Another pioneer for tofu is Thelma Dalman who is Director of Food Services in Santa Cruz, California, who supplies the schools and hospitals in that town with wholefood meals which include tofu dishes. She has eliminated sugar, food colourings and chemical additives from school lunches, and she supplies wholemeal bread from bakeries run by the school lunch programme to the schools. (In California, it is a law that every school-going child must be provided with a school meal.) Thelma Dalman has done a tremendous amount of work with the USDA (US Department of Agriculture) pointing out the advantages of tofu as a protein source in the school lunch programme. In 1978, she introduced tofu to this scheme and she has been using it since. Moreover, Thelma sends weekly menus to the parents listing what their children will be having in school meals and explaining policies. Since she brought about the change to more natural meals in the schools and hospitals, there has been a marked decrease in behavioural problems, especially among handicapped youngsters in hospitals who would normally be prone to difficult behaviour patterns.

All these people and many more are contributing to the growing popularity of tofu. Each year it seems that there are about 25 per cent more factories and businesses related to soyfoods than there were the year before. Consumption of tofu is growing by at least 25-30 per cent annually without any advertising campaigns, and this shows that people are becoming more aware of it. In this time of high unemployment, these figures would seem to offer encouragement to anyone who might be interested in starting his own factory or soy delicatessen. The media in America have certainly taken notice of the growth of the industry, and there have been articles in *The Wall Street Journal* and *The New York Times*, amongst others, to that effect. In the East, there are many tofu shops, something on the scale of bakeries in the USA or perhaps newsagents or fish and chip shops in these islands; and soon, hopefully, there will also be a significant number of tofu shops, tempeh factories, miso and natural soy sauce factories throughout England, Ireland and Europe.

FURTHER READING

Binding, G. J. *About Soya Beans*. Wellingborough, Northamptonshire: Thorsons Publishers Limited, 1980.

Davis, Adelle. *Let's Have Healthy Children*. Allen and Unwin, 1974.

Lappe, Frances Moore. *Diet for a Small Planet*. New York: Ballantine Books, 1976.

McGruter, Patricia Gaddis. *The Great American Tofu Cookbook*. Brookline, Massachusetts: Autumn Press, 1979. (Distributed by Thorsons.)

Shurtleff, William and Aoyagi, Akiko. *The Book of Miso*. Brookline, Massachusetts: Autumn Press, 1976. (Distributed by Thorsons.)

Shurtleff, William and Aoyagi, Akiko. *The Book of Tofu*. New York: Autumn Press, 1975. (Distributed by Thorsons.)

INDEX

Photograph of Jane O'Brien on back cover by Ursula Steiger.